Noble Enterprise

The Commonsense Guide to Uplifting People and Profits

Noble Enterprise

The Commonsense Guide to Uplifting People and Profits

DARWIN GILLETT

COSIMO

NEW YORK

Noble Enterprise: The Commonsense Guide to Uplifting People and Profits

For information, address:
P.O. Box 416, Old Chelsea Station
New York, NY 10011

or visit our website at:
www.cosimobooks.com

Ordering Information:
Cosimo publications are available at online bookstores. They may also be purchased for educational, business or promotional use:
- *Bulk orders:* special discounts are available on bulk orders for reading groups, organizations, businesses, and others. For details contact Cosimo Special Sales at the address above or at info@cosimobooks.com.
- *Custom-label orders:* we can prepare selected books with your cover or logo of choice. For more information, please contact Cosimo at info@cosimobooks.com.

Cover Design by www.popshopstudio.com

Cover photo: iStockPhoto.com/5392094/Maliketh

ISBN: 978-1-60520-118-4

To Barbara,
whose love and partnership I cherish

"The real voyage of discovery begins not in seeking new landscapes,
but in having new eyes."

—Marcel Proust

"What an exciting book! *Noble Enterprise* provides the reader with a profound and enlightened worldview that fundamentally changes the way we see the reality of corporate success. Real change begins when we correctly see the underlying factors. Author Dar Gillett offers a way of shifting values and leadership focus to create a more evolved way of doing business. He gives us a clear map of how to do just that and a stunning example demonstrating that it works!"

—Patricia B. Corbett, cofounder and president,
The Mindshift Institute (NY), past CEO of Griswold-
Bateman, an international distribution corporation

"Gillett's book pioneers a new area of crucial importance in managing knowledge-based companies. In his convincing presentation on *Noble Enterprise* and the emerging field of human economics, he brings us state-of-the-art thinking and challenges us to do better and be better."

—George Starcher, president,
European Baha'i Business Forum,
former senior partner,
McKinsey & Company (France)

"Gillett has chosen to focus on the human dynamics of business success—not on psychological gimmicks, manipulative programs, or sophistic explanations, but on the fundamentals that drive human performance and sustain it."

—Robert H. Schaffer, founder, Robert H. Schaffer &
Associates (CT), author of *The Breakthrough Strategy*

"Gillett just widened the goalposts for organizational success! His *Noble Enterprise* leverages the potential of human interaction in fostering sustainable corporate effectiveness."

—Jack F. Haren, president, Mohawk Fine Paper (NY)

"Darwin Gillett's *Noble Enterprise* shows you how you can bring the very best of who you are to your job rather than leaving it at the door. He has effectively linked the intersection between humanity and profits."

—Peter D. Moore, business strategy advisor,
founder, Snowmass Forum (CO)

"Sustainable business success requires building the right kind of human relationships—both within a company and with all of its constituencies. When those relationships—and the entire business—are powered by noble intentions, noble ethics, and noble actions, great things happen. People and companies become passionate about their work: fully alive, energized, and focused on what matters most. Gillett's book describes how leaders can build those relationships, and is illustrated by a great case example of a turnaround company. This book will change how we think about business, how we shape business relationships, and how we lead business. I'm recommending it to all my business clients. Gillett's vision of noble enterprise is a model for twenty-first-century business success."

—Joe Bavonese, PhD, codirector and cofounder of the Relationship Institue, and codirector of Uncommon Practices (MI)

"When an executive with hands-on business experience extols the benefits of ethical values and spiritual capital, take note and read! *Noble Enterprise* makes many of today's cutting-edge business concepts come pragmatically alive."

—David A. Schwerin, PhD, president, Institute for Ethical Awareness (PA), author of *Conscious Globalism: What's Wrong With the World and How to Fix It*

"*Noble Enterprise* is: No Bull. Noble. Nobel. Buy it and feed your Soul."

—Martin Rutte, coauthor, *Chicken Soup for the Soul at Work*

"The latest experiments in physics demonstrate that 'reality' is comprised of interconnected energy. This has profound ramifications for business and leadership. Dar Gillett has organized a set of business principles based on this energy view of reality and on his research of successful companies and their leaders. These clear and practical principles show ways to tap the full range of human energy (including the firm's Spiritual Capital) to improve the bottom line and employee job satisfaction and development."

—Barbara Williams, CEO, Image Content Technology, LLC (CT)

"International merger and acquisitions are fraught with danger. Overpaying for an asset is an obvious risk, but the challenge of true integration is an even greater one. Without cultural sensitivity and a clear vision, integration will fail, and value will be destroyed. Such a vision must have as its basis universal ethical standards, and the ability to enthuse the entire merged entity with energy. Dar Gillett's book *Noble Enterprise* delivers a framework that will allow business leaders to construct such a critical philosophy for all their stakeholders, through honesty, clarity, and belief. If you are serious about growing your business, you should read this book."

—Neil Collen, partner, Livingstone Partners (London)

"In *Noble Enterprise*, Dar Gillett talks about aspects of leadership that most people ignore and provides a concrete example of how lofty values can translate into powerful results. If your company needs to do things differently, this book might provide some fresh inspiration."

—Ron Ashkenas, managing partner, Robert H. Schaffer
& Associates (CT), coauthor of *The Boundaryless
Organization*, *The GE Work-Out*, and *Rapid Results*

"An outstanding guidebook for future start-up companies, their management, and the implementation of ethical standards."

—Dr. Klaus-Peter Reiner, former vice president, sales
and marketing, LONZA GmbH, managing director,
MWK GmbH (Germany)

"Dar Gillett in *Noble Enterprise* has gone far beyond a 'how to do it' book. It is the best 'who done it' book I've read in years, exciting in its tales of real-life characters and exciting events. It is profoundly personally relevant as it peels away the onion rings of each Noble Enterprise, leaving us to understand not only the keys to success, but in addition how that dose of tender loving care with which we approach the task makes for a great cake. Enjoy!"

—Dale Emerson, CEO, Archibel SA (Belgium)

"Dar Gillett deftly delves into the head and heart of this significant transformation effort. He has accurately captured the full impact of an inspirational leader on truly transforming a complex organization. This is a fascinating journey from cover to cover that provides both organizational and personal insights. Any change agent, in any organization, will find this useful, and all of us can learn what true leadership looks like."

—David Sissons, vice president,
Hay Group Insight and Reward Information
Services Canada—Hay Group (Canada)

"This book shows how we can be tough, disciplined business people *and* treat our employees like we want our sons, daughters, spouses, and ourselves treated. It tells the story of how one CEO combined science and soul to create a way for leaders to run a successful business, and to go home at night and be proud of not only *what* they did but also of *how* they did it. Dar Gillett does an excellent job of capturing not only the lessons and fundamentals of *how* to run a noble enterprise but also the intrinsic rewards it brings to visionary leaders who undertake this challenge."

—Renato Discenza, former vice president,
business transformation, AT&T Canada;
former senior vice president, Bell Canada

"We help people—whether employees of our businesses or citizens of our state—not merely by providing material benefits, but even more so by empowering them to become more and achieve more on their own. Gillett's *Noble Enterprise* embodies this truth and helps business owners and executives apply it in their businesses. Read it and uplift your people *and* your profits!"

—State Senator Paula Benoit, former owner of
Magnolia Gift Store and Baby Magnolia Children's
Clothing (Bath, Maine)

"Dar Gillett is uniquely qualified to write about the Noble Enterprise because he has spent years living and practicing these principles. Interconnection and collaboration have been major themes and priorities in his life and work. This book provides a new and more compassionate way of thinking about business and the human beings who function in it."

—Carol Coutrier, president and CEO, The Launching Pad & Co., president, Massachusetts Specialty Foods Association, and finalist for 1995 New England Women Business Owner's Business Woman of the Year Award

"Why are major corporations inviting poets, actors, painters, and symphony conductors to work with their senior leadership team? Because the traditional patterns of leadership simply aren't providing the results demanded by stakeholders. Gillett's *Noble Enterprise* provides the framework together with a concrete success story of how the leaders of one company not only revitalized their organization but achieved breakthrough performance. It is a must read for serious students and practitioners of leadership."

—Ken Bardach, associate dean and Charles and Joanne Knight Distinguished Director of Executive Programs, Olin Business School, Washington University in St. Louis

TABLE OF CONTENTS

FOREWORD

by Kenneth Bardach, associate dean and Charles and Joanne Knight
Distinguished Director of Executive Programs at Olin Business School,
Washington University in St. Louis

During the late 1980s, when I was associate dean at another leading business school, I had occasion to attend a dinner to honor an alumnus who had recently given the school a major gift.

When Jerry began his speech, he explained that he came from humble means, but despite the lack of money, his father frequently said, "When you have, you give." Throughout his career, Jerry had tried to follow this advice. And now that he was a successful trader with a seat on the NYSE, he was able to make a major donation to the school.

Jerry continued his speech by sharing an important personal observation: namely, that more and more people were trying to find "purpose and meaning" in their lives. Jerry explained further that he was one of the fortunate ones because he had found much "purpose and meaning" in his own life and career through many channels but principally through work—by helping to create and participate in organizations that were among the top in their field, and which at the same time brought a sense of "nobility" for all constituencies associated with them.

Something deep and profound resonated in me with this speech. I agreed with Jerry then and I believe it continues to this day that many of us are trying to find "purpose and meaning" in our lives. I think it has to do with our need to give, to serve, and ultimately to leave our mark of accomplishments that reflect having used our time in a creative, meaningful, and ethical manner. It is about making a difference...about contributing to some value or vision that connects to higher purpose within us that calls upon our best efforts and passionate resolve.

Darwin Gillett captures and explains this concept magnificently from the combined standpoint of an historian, philosopher, economist and business consultant in his new book, *Noble Enterprise*. He gives us the rationale, the framework, and the tools to design, build, and manage a Noble Enterprise: one that consistently outperforms its competition, in making profit, attracting and motivating the best talent in the field, and serving customers. While these characteristics often are viewed as conflicting, Gillett argues persuasively that attaining the three concurrently is not only attainable but is a requirement to create a sustainable profitable organization in today's rapidly changing, globally competitive environment.

Gillett divides *Noble Enterprise* into three main sections: Part I, "Energizing People and Their Companies"; Part II, "Revitalizing a Near-Death Company"; and Part III, "Origins of a New Corporation." While Part III, as in a good "whodunit," provides "the answers," Part II is in some ways the most interesting and inspiring of the three in that it features the fascinating case of the revitalization of Unitel (renamed AT&T Canada Long Distance Services in the process), and then extracts from this case the "principals" necessary to create a Noble Enterprise. And Part I is a must read not only to understand the challenges and issues but also because of the useful management insights and perspectives Gillett provides.

From the very outset Gillett makes clear that the book centers around the integration of values and performance; more specifically, about aligning values of the individual with those of the organization and ultimately with a consistent and compelling mission and strategy. In sum, it's not only about what one accomplishes, but also about *how* one does it.

In Chapter 1, Gillett relates the story of his first meeting with Bill Catucci, the CEO of AT&T Canada LDS, during Catucci's last day on the job: Gillett asked Catucci what was the key to the turnaround, and Catucci replied: "It's not one thing. It's everything. You have to do everything. But it's also about *how* you do it." He pointed to the immense untapped wisdom and spirit of people within any organization, and the CEO's responsibility to get people engaged, aware of how much they can contribute, and excited about helping the company succeed…. "With all the talk about technology, business strategy, and high finance, it's so easy for CEOs to lose sight of the fact that it is *people* who make the difference. How simple it really is. But it takes more than *knowing* it, or *talking* about it—it takes *doing* it!"

One of the important insights early in Part I is the positive relationship between employee morale and profitability. As Gillett explains from an interview with Catucci, "They [top management] view employee morale as something nice to have, but expendable when it comes to the desire to increase profits. They don't realize that it is one of the key drivers of business strength and profitability. When a company is so low in morale, how can it possibly compete with the leaders?" It's one thing to understand this relationship, it's another to internalize its importance, and still another to do it. One of the major benefits of *Noble Enterprise* is Gillett's detailed discussion and analysis of how top management can systematically build and sustain employee morale and then leverage these gains to generate outstanding operational and financial performance. Consistent with Catucci's statement, Gillett embraces the concept that employee morale is more than a "nice-to-have." It's an increasingly key driver of business success.

Recognizing, linking, and harmonizing the dichotomy between profitable performance—what Gillett calls, "the Hard Stuff," "the Outer Dimension," "Action"—with employee morale—referred to as "the Soft Stuff," "the Inner Dimension," "Being"—is a major focus of the book. Gillett argues that "often missing is the *inner dimension* which is a direct and necessary counterpart to (and fuel of) the outer dimension." Gillett poses and then explains the following questions: Why do most organizations tend to focus in such large measure on "the Outer Dimension"? Why is it so important to focus on both? Why is so hard to incorporate "the Inner Dimension"? What are the costs of not doing so? What are best practices to support "best being" and thereby generate rather than sabotage superior performance?

In general the book reads easily even though the concepts are complex. It is a credit to Gillett that he has been able break complexity down into bite-size morsels without diluting or oversimplifying the authenticity or completeness of the analysis. And his tables and pictorial descriptions are excellent. A case in point: "The Five Pillars of a Noble Enterprise," shown as a classical Greek temple with five columns set upon a base of "human energies" and representing "larger purpose, ethical values, human growth, freedom, and unity" to support the dome labeled "the Noble Enterprise." The Five Pillars provide the framework to build a Noble Enterprise from the ground up, a challenge Gillett addresses methodically in Chapter 13.

For me, Gillett's most interesting and innovative thinking is found in

Part III, beginning with Chapter 12, "A Human Economics." Gillett explains cogently here the differences between "Material Economic Reality," the paradigm that has historically driven management methods and behavior, and "Human Economic Reality," the emerging model. He summarizes the differences by pointing out that in Material Economics, financial capital drove the wealth creation process through the purchase of plant and equipment and the financing of material inventories; the human ingredient, primarily labor, was expensed and expendable; and people were seen as and accounted and managed as a "commodity." In contrast, in a time of Human Economics, it is human capital that drives the wealth creation process; financial capital is "purchased" by companies with strong Human Capital; and the "commodity" here is financial capital. This poignant differentiation helps to explain why companies sometimes talk about "people being their most important asset" while behaving very differently. Namely, during periods of adversity, leadership is unable to maintain the transition from Material Economics to Human Economics.

Another interesting ramification of this distinction is Gillett's explanation that managers operating in a Human Economics mindset "concentrate on inspiring people with a compelling corporate purpose and ethical values." They focus on the knowledge and inner energies that people bring to work. In this regard, I am reminded of Jack Welch's prescient assertion during the early 1990s that the role of management was shifting from winning the hands of the worker, to winning the mind of the worker, to winner the soul of the worker. Also, I am reminded of frequent comments by many well-known CEOs about the enormous time they spend interviewing for new hires at relatively low levels of the organization. Why would they "waste their time" in such behavior? In Gillett's framework, "they seek to optimize the inner dimension, i.e. human energies, for example, hiring for attitude, not just knowledge and experience." Later, Gillett talks about the importance of cultural fit—an apt shorthand for values alignment.

Later in Chapter 12, Gillett develops yet another fascinating framework based on what he calls "Three Economic Ages": the Industrial Age, the Information Age, and the Relationship Age. In the Relationship Age companies recognize the power of human relationships "not merely to get customers or to create collaborative relationships but as a business model."

As another dimension of the Relationship Age, "management recognizes and invites the full array of human energy to work, not just the energies of the body and mind but also the energies of the human spirit. In other words, Relationship Age companies add Spiritual Capital to the financial and intellectual capital needed to gain competitive capital."

The ensuing discussion of Spiritual Capital is perhaps the most compelling and transforming part of *Noble Enterprise*. In it, Gillett makes a compelling case that Spiritual Capital is "the energy of Human Spirit which, when fully expressed in service to the highest good for all those connected with and affected by the company, fuels corporate success in its broadest sense."

During most of the post–WWII period, we in business schools have built our curriculum upon the scientific method as manifest through faculty research. As a result, our MBAs tended to be highly intelligent men and women with excellent analytical stills. However, in the 1980s, industry leadership began complaining that these men and women often lacked team and collaborative skills; they knew how to solve problems but they didn't know how to select good problems to solve; they lacked solid ethical footings; they lacked commitment to the historical financial goals and aspirations of the organization.

Overall, the response to these criticisms has been sincere but tentative: new leadership and ethics courses, more experiential learning, more action learning and internships with business so that the new graduates could adapt their new knowledge and skills more quickly and effectively to the needs of the organization.

But only recently have business schools begun to recognize the importance of expanding their mindset beyond Intellectual Capital to include the development of Spiritual Capital. The "Sustainability" curriculum has moved beyond fringe to mainstream as students prepare to work for companies that truly believe in "doing well by doing good" and in product and service innovation to capture underdeveloped economic markets. Today, many companies seek young talent with high purpose, ethical values, a caring and respectful attitude toward customers and fellow employees, and a respect for the community and the environment at large.

How do business schools teach such qualities—or at least provide people with such values, knowledge, insights, and tools needed to make a significant positive contribution to their future employers? The answer, I believe, is to bring "Spiritual Capital" into the curriculum, although not always by this name and not always in the traditional course venue.

It's exciting. It's beginning to happen. And to this end, Darwin Gillett's *Noble Enterprise* is an important and potentially transforming contribution for students entering the workforce, for practicing executives who want to expand and ennoble their organizations—and achieve superior business performance in the process—and for those of us with the responsibility and pleasure of providing our students with new and impactful ideas.

INTRODUCTION
A Revolution—From the Inside Out

M any years ago, Bob Moore, then controller of Union Camp, a major U.S. paper and forest products company later acquired by International Paper, brought me in as a consultant to help him create a more cohesive, collaborative organization. One aspect of this work was to design and help facilitate periodic working conferences of his geographically dispersed organization. After one such conference, as we debriefed, Bob suddenly observed, "Dar, you're always talking about *energy*!" He was right. While most observers would have described the conference in terms of who said and did what and what was decided, I was seeing the "action" in terms of the *energies* behind those words and actions.

I had started out my career in the material/financial dimension of business. With degrees in economics and business and strengths in mathematics, I had gravitated to the quantitative side of business. I did financial analysis, built financial models, and saw business in terms of economics. I had helped develop a business planning system for my employer (Union Carbide, then a 95,000-person Fortune 50 manufacturer of chemicals and plastics), and then later consulted to major corporations on business strategy development.

However the interchange with Bob Moore made me conscious of how differently I was seeing the work environment and the nature of my real help to clients. It had been just natural to me, and thus subconscious. Others see form—certain behaviors, certain results—and thus focus on manipulating those forms. But I had begun seeing that form is the *result* of energy: the energy of motivations, of feelings, of perceptions. Thus I naturally focused on and worked with those energies. What I found was that when the energies were right, then the desired outer actions would happen and the desired results would be achieved—sometimes results even beyond the desired results.

While working with or consulting to companies of different sizes and industries and at different levels within them, I continually sought universal principles of business, organization, and leadership, particularly those that transcended compartmentalization and that offered a unified approach. Looking beyond just their products, markets, and technologies, I began to experience these companies as energy fields. I began seeing the role of those energies in the success or failure of the companies I observed.

Earlier, while still in the traditional phase of my career, I worked with senior management teams on issues of corporate direction and business strategy. This work often involved designing and leading planning conferences for senior executives. At the time, I thought the success of these conferences (and my being referred into other companies as a result) came from my intellectual abilities regarding business strategy. Later, reflecting back, I realized that what many of the executive participants were getting out of these conferences was not so much due to my intellectual contributions regarding business strategy, as it was due to their (often new) experience of working collaboratively with other senior executives, and that I had played a constructive role in that.

Thus despite my early quantitative bent, I gradually became more conscious of the importance of the human dimension, including the spiritual aspect of people and of organizations. In the early 1980s I became involved in what is now known as corporate social responsibility and spirit at work. This started with my organizing and leading—with my minister—a group of business executives in exploring the idea of applying one's Christian principles in business, which in turn led to my giving talks on Heart Power at several churches and at a strategic planning association conference. I then began giving talks with Gordon Davidson of the Center for Visionary Leadership on the energies of successful corporations for human resource and organization development associations.

I began focusing my exploration on finding answers to questions including:

1. How do these two worlds—one a material world and the other a human energy world—interrelate?
2. In what way do they need to be balanced, integrated, and made into one whole?
3. And how can leaders most effectively deal with the two dimensions?

The more I pondered these questions, the more I felt that "business as usual" was not adequately addressing those questions. In the early 1990s

I began contemplating a book that would delve into these questions and present a new business model. Several early versions described an Energized Enterprise, powered by the full range of human energies. Whereas business traditionally has welcomed and utilized first physical energy and then subsequently mental energy, it was still struggling with emotional energy and seemed blind to the power of heart energy and conflicted about will energy. When I saw *Fortune* magazine's cover story article in the mid 1990s describing a "new" type of capital—Intellectual Capital—described by Thomas Stewart, I knew then that what I was exploring was essentially Spiritual Capital, including the energies that business had not yet incorporated in its model, namely the energies of Heart, Will, and Emotions. Thus the power driving the Energized Enterprise was not only Intellectual Capital, but also Spiritual Capital.

Though several publishers were intrigued and interested in the book, the project waned, in large part because I wanted to find some vivid examples of my concepts in practice. That opportunity came one January morning in 1999, when I met Bill Catucci, who had just led the dramatic revitalization of a Canadian telecommunications company. That story became not only an example of the energized enterprise at work, but (as I began to realize while interviewing people involved in the turnaround) it also demonstrated the power of nobility in inspiring people and driving positive change and greater business performance. I quickly wrote an article about it[†] and decided to make it a major part of my book.

On one level this book is about how to make a business far more successful by paying attention to the inner power of people and organizations catalyzed by working toward higher, more inspiring goals and working together in a spirit of unity and connection.

On a higher level, the book is about a possible future of (or, some would say, successor to traditional) Capitalism—a change that might usher in a new wave not only of economic growth and development, but also of expanding human spiritual development and rising well-being.

In both cases it is about a shift in individual consciousness (and motivation) from an earlier time when physical survival and eventually material well-being were the only objectives of participants. This new consciousness

---

† "Bringing a Company Back to Life: The Role of a CEO," available at www. NoleBusinessSolutions.com

reflects an emerging inner, spiritually based view of human development, of corporate strategy and of markets.

Maslow's hierarchy of needs depicts mankind's evolution from a lower drive for survival to a higher drive for self-actualization. Capitalism in its broadest sense reflects the average level of human consciousness. To be successful and effectively motivate people, Capitalism has the opportunity to embrace and reflect humanity's shift from a physical survival mode to a self-actualized mode. Hence the need to add nobility to the business world—namely the aspiration to serve a high purpose, to act ethically, and to recognize and honor the deep interconnection we have with each other and the earth, and to hardwire this into the concept of the business enterprise… a shift that can add value for company employees and the broader community in addition to the shareholders and effectively attract and motivate employees and increase profits.

Our economic system must evolve to meet the changing needs and aspirations of humanity. More and more people are demanding that their work experience be fulfilling and beneficial to the world at large. The best employees, who enjoy multiple employment opportunities, insist upon it. The companies that see this reality and adapt to it will be most open to embracing the concept of the Noble Enterprise—to help them create sustainable competitive advantage.

Thus, this book is about human evolution that is increasingly involving the spiritual dimension of life, one that is taking place within individual people, within companies, and within Capitalist societies. My intent in writing it is to speak to both those who already see this more humane (perhaps even spiritual) side of business and also to those steeped in the financial and economic dimension of business who may be more hesitant about changing the business model, with a book that shows how both dimensions (of people and finance) together make up the whole that is needed for companies and the people associated with them to survive and thrive in the future.

I offer *Noble Enterprise* as a model not only for shaping and leading companies to greater success, but also potentially for rewiring marketplaces, industries, and whole economies as Noble Enterprises serving the highest good for all participants, not just the material good of a few.

The purpose of *Noble Enterprise* at the first level—that of individual business operations and performance—is to bring together into one unified model of the corporation two apparently conflicting aspects of business: the (outer) material (or "financial") dimension and the (inner) human energy dimension. Dualistic thinking about the material and human energy dimensions of business triggers apparent dichotomies such as the view that we have to choose between people or profits. One of the central messages of this book is that it is *both* people *and* profit. They are intricately intertwined, and by focusing on both people and profit simultaneously, we enhance both.

By focusing on just one, we do harm to the whole company and, paradoxically, do not necessarily even achieve progress on that one dimension. For example, focusing only on profits and ignoring the human dimension may create some short-term gains, but they will not likely be sustainable if the human dimension is being minimized. Conversely, focusing only on the human dimension without directly connecting it to business performance and the resulting financial performance fails to utilize whatever gains in the human dimension may be created.

Everything is an interactive energy field, including this book. Occasionally, people ask me, "Where did these ideas come from?" They seem to want an answer like: "Oh, it's based on the work of so-and-so (as described in his/her book *X*)". The answer "It just came to me" doesn't seem good enough for them. It's a fascinating question, actually, for is anything ever really new? I could say in truth that the book is all based on my experience working with business clients and observing companies and their leaders and organizations. But the process of writing the book was not simply a memory dump to get it all on paper. No, it was more of a dialogue between me and, well, the book, I would have to say. When I came up against a place where I knew there was something more to be said, but did not know what it was, I found myself just asking—and then waiting, and invariably, an answer came to me. Was it the *book* teaching *me*?

Design and Flow of the Book

In Chapter 1, we meet Bill Catucci and learn about the remarkable corporate revitalization he led of Unitel, a failing Canadian telecommunications company. This sets the stage for exploring what enables some companies to succeed while others, despite Herculean efforts, do not.

The rest of Part I addresses the energy dimension of work organizations. It looks at the energy of motivated workers, exploring the realm of nonmaterial motivators. It looks at the energies of effective organizations, encouraging a perspective of energy flow regarding what makes some companies sick and failing and some companies healthy and vibrant. It identifies the specific energies of vibrant organizations and provides guidelines for building vibrant organizations.

Part II tells the story of Unitel/AT&T Canada Long Distance Services and how its leader tapped and unleashed its human energies to power a dramatic corporate revitalization. We see the revitalization of human energy as well as the revitalization of financial performance. Simultaneously morale goes from one of the worst of five hundred North American companies tracked by the Hay Group to one of the best in just three years, and the financial value of the company grows fivefold. This section shows how a company can be revitalized when management tends to both the *inner* and *outer* drivers of business performance. But I intended this story to do more than just show and instruct. I wanted you to see and feel the inner shifts people made and to use it as a source of inspiration as you set out to take your business (and your leadership) to a higher level, for such a transformation takes not only the tools (and Best Practices) but also the desire, the passion, and the courage ("Best Energies"?) to use them successfully.

Part III takes a fresh look at economics, the corporation, and leadership in light of the human energy dimension. Business operates within a larger context of reality, what we like to call the "real world." That real world has been changing before our eyes, as quantum physics changes our understanding of the laws of reality, and as an emerging spiritual perspective is experienced by a growing percentage of North American society. With a fresh view of a practical reality that includes both the material and energy dimensions, we define a broadened view of economics, human capital, corporate success, leadership, the common good, and the change process.

I hope this book provides some useful ideas to you for making your company more successful and making you a more fulfilled and effective leader—and especially that it inspires you and your colleagues to blaze your own noble path to that future.

Darwin Gillett
www.NobleBusinessSolutions.com
Phippsburg, Maine
April 2008

PART I

ENERGIZING PEOPLE AND THEIR COMPANIES

CHAPTER 1

AN UNCOMMON TURNAROUND

In my quest to find examples of companies that were consciously working to energize the Human Spirit as well as the mind, I visited Toronto in January 1999 and met over breakfast with the CEO of a small company. As I shared my vision of the role of Human Spirit in successful companies, his face brightened, and he said, "You know, you really should meet Bill Catucci. Bill is CEO of AT&T Canada Long Distance Services. He's done just what you're talking about. But you won't meet him this trip because today is his last day. He's retiring today."

After breakfast, Don and I walked to his office building. We happened to run into Bill Catucci as he was walking through the lobby. Don introduced us and, turning to Bill, said, "I told Dar he needed to meet you. He's writing a book about just the kind of inspiring, humanistic management approach that you have used. I know he'd like to hear about what you've done here."

A tall, large-framed man with an engaging smile, Bill greeted me with the contagious enthusiasm and warmth of a man enjoying life. I anticipated a short exchange of pleasantries and then he would hurry off to stay on his undoubtedly busy last-day schedule. He responded before I even had time to think about how I might contact him later. "Sure. What better day than my last day on the job! Come on into my office."

Entering his office, I wondered how he had time to meet with a complete stranger. I said I did not want to impose on this important day.

"I purposely kept the schedule open," Bill replied. "Schedules too often become a trap for CEOs. They cram their schedules full. It's like a Linus blanket. It makes them feel important. Plus, it can be threatening to have spare time. CEOs should allow empty places in their schedules for unexpected things. I make sure I have some unscheduled time to meet with people on short notice or to deal with issues of the day, rather than be trapped in schedules."

Immediately, I was intrigued. Emboldened, I asked him about the company.

He started with, "It's a long story with lots of components," then launched into a description of the exciting three years that were just ending. "First, you have to understand what shape this company was in when I got involved. Unitel [the predecessor company] was losing a million dollars a day. Its strategy hadn't been working. It had lost market share. Its costs were eating it alive. Its quality was inadequate. Customers were leaving. Top sales people had left. The management team had mostly left. And, I discovered, not surprisingly, that the morale of the 2600 remaining people was in the pits. The several companies that owned this company had been at odds with each other. The strategy kept changing. And the CEO position had been a revolving door.

"That's what I inherited. I called it a 'company in trauma.' But now, three years later, the company has excellent quality, strong customer service, greater market share, and is worth several times what it was worth three years ago—as valued by an outside financial company. And we improved employee morale in the process."

"How did you turn it around?" I asked.

"First of all, this was not just my doing. It took visionary people at both AT&T and the three major Canadian banks—Bank of Nova Scotia, the Royal Bank of Canada, and Toronto Dominion—who held the debt of the company to agree on a new strategy, to create a new ownership structure, and to provide a fresh financial capital infusion, despite the company's gigantic losses and weak industry position. The banks also converted some of their existing debt to equity.

"I was extremely fortunate that AT&T and the banks had the confidence in me to select me as CEO—someone who had never even *been* a CEO before. Plus the owners and the Board provided me with the support and resources to do the job that needed to be done. And I did not do it alone. I was blessed with an outstanding leadership team and a truly wonderful group of employees—and together we revitalized this company.

"Furthermore, it is fashionable when entering a new job to ascribe all the past and even continuing failures to one's predecessors. I reject this. My predecessors at Unitel were talented and hardworking leaders who were facing a far different situation than mine. I had the good fortune to benefit from the foundation they laid, which enabled me to succeed."

Bill recalled the new vision he had created for the company and how its mission had attracted the talent and resources needed to fuel the turnaround, about how the company's employees themselves defined the company's values, and how they had found powerful ways to build those values into the fabric of the company's decision-making and reward systems.

"What was the key to the turnaround?" I asked.

"It wasn't one thing," he replied. "It was everything. You have to do everything. But it's also about *how* you do it." He pointed to the immense untapped wisdom and spirit of people within any organization and the CEO's responsibility to get people engaged, aware of how much they can contribute, and excited about helping the company succeed.

He described the governance system he had created, which kept management focused on the strategic issues of the company and working in *collaboration* rather than in the kind of *internal competition* prevalent in most large companies. He shared the business measures his team created, not just the traditional financial measures, but also other equally important drivers of business performance that captured the health of the people side of the business.

He provided vignettes of employees getting turned on and empowered. He told of times when he teamed up with sales people to reach the CEOs of large potential clients. He described how they used crises as a way of focusing energies and turning adversity into advantage, and how they had used celebrations as a way to reinforce positive accomplishments and to empower employees.

Bill held up a folder of congratulatory letters several inches thick. "Some of these are from employees. Some are from their families. Some are from customers. Some are even from competitors and government officials. The question I have is: *How will the people involved in this turnaround remember what has happened over these past three years? Sure, they see the results. But will they truly understand and remember how we did it? Or will the methods get lost in history, so that future leaders regress back to outdated management techniques?*"

Bill's assistant, Alice Coleman, entered. Bill introduced us. She told him about the plans for his retirement reception in the lobby and informed him that the legal department wanted to meet with him before that. I started to gather my coat and briefcase, but he motioned me to stay.

Alice left. Seemingly oblivious to the mundane issues of time scheduling, Bill observed, "This was my first CEO position. I always thought of myself as a *contrarian.* The stock answers and approaches never were enough for me. Down deep, I really *did* know that a whole new approach to leading a company would work. So much of it has to do with empowering people. With all the talk about technology, business strategy, and high finance, it's so easy for a CEO to lose sight of the fact that it is *people* who make the difference. How simple it really is. But it takes more than *knowing* it, or *talking* about it—it takes *doing* it!"

Several times, phone calls interrupted our conversation as people called to wish him well. One came from the leader of the company's union. After Bill finished, he explained that when he had come onboard, the union had intense resentment toward and mistrust of the company. "I inherited several thousand grievances. Working with the union was one of many things I had to do for the company to succeed. And you know what? Now they want *me* to be their candidate for CEO of another company that has major problems working with their union!"

Members of the legal department then filed in. They took out small pieces of paper and read a poem in tribute to their boss. I could see Bill drinking in their warm appreciation and radiating it back to them. This heartfelt interchange of energy was over in a moment, but the image lasted in my mind. He thanked each one of them as they left.

Afterward, Bill commented, "This is why people work together—to accomplish important goals together and to share moments of appreciation for the years of mutual respect and collaboration. You know, after today, I will likely never again see most of the people of this company. That's a hard thing to acknowledge."

The time flew. I said to him, "This story of what you have done here has to be told. It's so inspiring."

"But it's not a story about *me*," Bill replied. "It's a story about how a *company* can be turned around, if you focus on what's important and you involve people in the right way. It's a story about a different kind of leadership from the traditional approaches to running a company. It's a story about the turnaround of *people*, because ultimately the people *are* the company."

"What were the results of all this?" I asked.

"We built a far stronger telecommunications network," Bill responded. "We introduced new products. We improved product quality and customer service. Eventually, we were able to put the AT&T name on the company—the first time AT&T ever put its name on a company it did not wholly own. We won back customers who had left us and attracted other customers who had become entrenched with the competition. Our market share increased. We reduced losses dramatically, and the value of the company grew several fold."

"One of the most important things we did was rebuild employee morale." Bill put in front of me some charts from the survey of employees' opinions on a wide range of topics, including their level of respect for the company's management and their level of satisfaction and commitment. "These were developed by the Hay Group, a human resource consulting firm that tracks five hundred North American companies. We were near the bottom three years ago. Here's how we improved each year," Bill enthused as he pored over the report with me. "By our third year, we were above the top ten percent of the companies on just about all categories."

"This is an amazing story," I observed. "It starts from a company that is weak from so many perspectives and proceeds to a company that is strong on many fronts, in just three years. Other companies would pay big bucks to get that kind of employee morale and commitment."

Overall Results: Yankee Group Report Card

Performance Objective	Level of Performance	
	Prior Grade at Start	Rating After Two Years
Improve Quality	F	A
Streamline Operations	F	B+
Improve Morale	D-	B
Improve Customer Satisfaction	C-	B+
Improve Financial Performance	C	B+
Move Toward Profitability	F	A+
Change Market Perception	D+	A
Overcome Ownership Uncertainty	C	A
Overall Grade	D	A-

In late November 1997, two years into the turnaround, The Yankee Group, a telecommunications consulting firm, did an in-depth analysis of the company and generated a "report card" on AT&T Canada. The chart shows how The Yankee Group had rated Unitel at the start of the turnaround and then two years later.

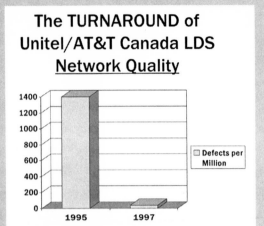

The TURNAROUND of Unitel/AT&T Canada LDS
Network Quality

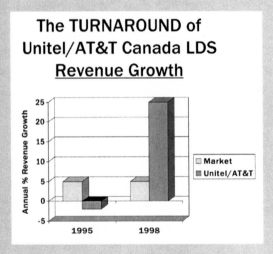

The TURNAROUND of Unitel/AT&T Canada LDS
Revenue Growth

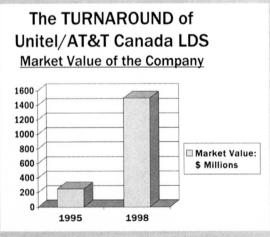

The TURNAROUND of Unitel/AT&T Canada LDS
Market Value of the Company

The TURNAROUND of
Unitel/AT&T Canada LDS
Employee Morale: 1995 ->1998

Legend:
☐ Unitel: 1994/5 % below Ave
■ AT&T: 1998 % above Ave

Categories (x-axis): Corp Direction, Communications, Recognition, Management Style, Emp Satisfaction, Commit to Emp, Comp & Ben

Source: Hay Group

Survey categories included employees' feelings about: corporate direction, communications, performance management, performance emphasis, job stress, recognition, training & development, management style, management image, employee involvement, supervision, employee satisfaction & commitment, operating efficiency & productivity, commitment to employees, quality & customer service, and compensation & benefits.

"But often they don't focus on that," Bill replied. "They view it as something nice to have but less important than the desire to increase profits. For me, it was one of the key drivers of business strength and profitability. When a company is so low in morale, how can it possibly compete with the leaders?"

"I don't want to make this sound easy," Bill continued. "It's not. When I came here, the employees must have thought, 'Here comes another CEO from the States—the fourth in five years. What magic wand will he try to wave? Who will he bring with him from the States? We'll just sit back and watch this one leave after a few months.' That's the reality. You don't just come in here and say, 'Everything's going to be great because I say so,' and everyone salutes and falls in step. There is skepticism, cynicism, and at the very best, a wait-and-see attitude."

"So, how did you do this?" I asked.

"First of all, *I* didn't do it. *We* all did it together. But as the CEO, you've got to lead, and that means first earning people's trust. You've got to create a vision, then sell it. You've got to set the company's values and then live them—not just when it's easy, but when it really matters. When you do that, people begin to listen. They begin to get on board. And they begin to feel good about being part of a company that stands for something good, that is trying to be the best, and that values its employees. I wanted our employees to get up in the morning, look at themselves in the mirror, and say, 'I want to go to work today because I believe in this company and what it stands for, and because I know what my role is in making it the best it can be.'"

Alice ducked her head into the office. "It's time for your reception." Bill got up and invited me to come with him. As we rode the elevator down to the lobby, we made arrangements to get together after his retirement. When the doors opened, Bill was swallowed in a sea of people.

The vast lobby was jammed with people. Hundreds of employees and well-wishers turned to welcome their leader. Bill moved into the crowd. *Oh, my God. I didn't expect this,* he thought. Hundreds clapped and cheered, with warm smiles and bright faces. They were gathered yet again in this space for one of many of the company's celebrations. Today, they honored their leader. The company had indeed turned around, and Bill had been selected as a finalist for Canadian CEO of the year. Three years earlier, many of these people were about to lose their jobs. Now they had not only their jobs, but also the pride of accomplishment and the joy of working with colleagues they cared about.

Bill made his way across the lobby. The applause rose, continuing even after he reached the front of the lobby. The air was electric. I could imagine Bill feeling the genuine warmth of the people he had just recently described to me. His few prepared remarks now seemed inadequate to him. When Bill spoke to groups, he always tried to say something a little funny, a little self-deprecating, like "Only my mother feels quite this way about me." How would he handle such an emotional moment? Could he find the right thing to say? How could any words be right in this situation?

Rick Waugh, the vice chairman of the Bank of Nova Scotia, the lead lending bank, presented Bill with a plaque of appreciation signed by the chairmen of all three banks. Rick joked that such unanimity was pretty much unheard of in the banking industry. In this case, he reminded everyone, the banks had been spared big write-offs and had instead realized a several hundred percent return on their investment in the company.

One by one, Bill's executive team members came up to the microphone to say their words of thanks to the CEO who had led them from near death to a prominent position in the industry. Judy McLeod, the senior vice president of Human Resources pinned the AT&T Canada LDS service pin on Bill's lapel. She said, "At the first meeting I had with Bill, we discussed implementing the service anniversary pins. It was Bill's idea to make them, not mine. Then for the next six months, he bugged me to get a pin for employees who retire. Now I know what he was really up to. He was planning his retirement, and he wanted one of these pins."

Finally, it was time for Bill to speak. Bill reached the podium and looked out at the people he had grown so fond of over the last three years. Three years ago, they were disillusioned and disheartened. But today, Bill felt the warmth and strength from their pride, their confidence, and their positive attitude. As he prepared to speak, an insight flashed through his mind. *This is what I truly wanted out of my career. I had thought I was here just to turn a company around, but now I realize it was for more than that. The ultimate for me is to touch people's lives and make them better. These people in front of me, who were down and out three years ago, now feel better about themselves and what they can achieve and believe in themselves. That is enough.*

People quieted to hear their CEO speak to them one last time. "Usually, I'm not at a loss for words…" People laughed. "…but this is a moment of mixed feelings for me. I've known most of you for at most only three years. Yet I feel I've known you far longer. We've had a lot of fun together making this company one of the best. And we did it in a different way from most corporations. We truly went down the 'road less traveled.'

"When I first arrived here, I wanted to make Unitel the finest long-distance company in Canada. I now realize that I had set my sights too low. With employees like you, you have not only made it the finest company in Canada but in North America and around the globe. And I have our employee survey to prove it.

"After three wonderful years, I will return to the U.S. with a fuller appreciation of the greatness of this country and its people. And, wherever I am, there will always be a place in my heart for the wonderful people of AT&T Canada LDS.

"You have a lot to be proud of. This company is one of the leading companies in Canada. Who would have thought that possible just three years ago? One of the main reasons is because of the kind of people standing right here. I see people of integrity, people of good will, people who respect others, and people who truly care about customers. Keep vigilant about our values. Keep nurturing that spirit that we created together."

Then it was over. But no one left. One by one, people came up to Bill to share a final moment with their leader. They shared memories and good wishes for each other. Each person delivered his or her words of heartfelt thanks to the leader they respected and liked, a leader who had helped them grow and contribute their best. People lingered, wanting to enjoy the good feelings as long as they could before they went back to their everyday work.

Standing in the back, despite being an outsider, I could feel the genuine warmth and connection between the leader and the employees. Here was a CEO who had worn his heart on his sleeve and put his heart and soul into his work. Now, at this celebration, it was being reflected back to him. I thought about what Bill had shared with me just moments earlier, the obvious pride he took in what he did to revive an organization, the letters he received from so many people who thanked him for what he had done, and his desire for the corporate revitalization to live on.

How had he and his organization pulled off this remarkable turnaround? And what were these new leadership approaches that he kept referring to?

Later, when we met to talk further about the story, Bill told me, "I think people should remember what we did here and how. It's too easy for these things to fade in people's memories."

That is our purpose for this book: to awaken the memories and insights too often hidden deep within ourselves of what can be and how to do it.

Later in the book (Part II), we will follow the journey that Bill and his colleagues took of corporate and personal transformation—a journey that turned a company and its people into winners. But first, in the next two chapters, we will look at why companies so often falter and fail to achieve the kinds of gains evident in the AT&T Canada LDS turnaround, and then we'll explore the five energies of highly successful companies like this one.

CHAPTER 2

WHY COMPANIES STRUGGLE

"The current problems we face cannot be solved at the same level of thinking with which they were created."

—Albert Einstein

"The real voyage of discovery begins not in seeking new landscapes, but in having new eyes."

—Marcel Proust

Why isn't the story of AT&T Canada run-of-the-mill? Why can't companies sustain steady improvement, growth, and success? Is it that some companies and their leaders are just not working hard enough? Or is it that they are following the wrong strategies? Or having difficulties in implementation? Or not hiring the right people and organizing their work well? Or not employing the latest improvement programs? Or not motivating and rewarding their people effectively? Or is it something else?

For some companies, these are indeed the reasons they are failing. But many of the companies that do address these problems also continue to struggle. Why do their efforts fail to yield the desired outcomes?

Common Strategies for Business Improvement

Let's look at some of the more common approaches for improving business performance, the premises that underlie them, and why they are often not enough by themselves to bring about the kind of dramatic improvements in performance that happened at Unitel/AT&T Canada:

1. Create the Grand New STRATEGY

    Premise: Performance is lackluster because we don't have the best strategy. So we redefine our business strategy for creating competitive advantage, such as mounting an acquisition program or repositioning ourselves vis-à-vis competition.

But what about those companies like Unitel/AT&T Canada that manage to turn around business performance without (as we will see in Part II) the strategy deemed best by outside experts? Coming up with the "grand strategy" often becomes a seductive path for CEOs, gaining them esteem with their colleagues as industry visionaries but not necessarily leading to improved performance.

2. Get into the right MARKET

Premise: Our profit and growth problems stem from not being in the right market, so let's get into more lucrative markets and industries where we can achieve growth and profitability more easily. "The grass is greener" somewhere else.

But what about all those companies that do succeed in mundane markets, crowded with competitors? How do they do it?

3. Get the best TECHNOLOGY

Premise: Technology, by providing better product or service features and more efficient and effective processes, is the source of competitive advantage.

What about companies that succeed even without the best technology? And, even if you do obtain the best technology, what enables your organization to capitalize on it?

4. Hire the BEST PEOPLE

Premise: Put the best people in the right positions and the rest takes care of itself. Get rid of the dead wood (Jack Welch urged companies to drop the bottom ten percent), then the remaining people will bring about improved performance, and our company will soar.

That's great, but plenty of companies do quite well even without hiring the "cream of the crop." Consider that in both the Unitel/AT&T Canada turnaround (Part II) and a subsequent one that CEO Bill Catucci led at Equifax, he purposely kept the people he inherited, often promoting them. Against the advice of some, he tapped the talent already there to achieve two back-to-back turnarounds.

5. Cut COSTS

Premise: Get costs (back) in line with revenues. With lower costs (and the *same* or better revenues), we'll make greater profits.

That's what the simple math says, but what if, by cutting costs, we also happen to be jeopardizing revenues, with the possible result of "cost-cutting our way out of business?" This had been the prior strategy of Unitel when Bill Catucci came on board.

6. Fix the Broken PARTS of the business

Premise: If we fix those parts of the company that are not functioning well (divisions, departments, business functions), then the whole company will function well.

This strategy stems from a view of the corporation as a machine. If it's not running well, then we have to find the part(s) that is/are broken and just fix it/them. But what if the "machine" isn't up to the job even when it's running well? What about the interaction between the parts? And what if by the very act of viewing the company as a machine we actually limit our ability to get it performing better?

7. Solve the Company's Biggest PROBLEMS

Premise: "Problems" stand in the way of our operating at peak performance. So if we find and eliminate or reduce those problems, the company will then reach a higher level of performance. So, just find out what's wrong, and fix it.

This is similar to the Fix the Parts Syndrome. It sounds reasonable to focus our energies on the problem areas. (Certainly someone should be doing that.) But if the very process of looking for (and fixing) problems then causes a climate of fear and failure, those "problems" may actually become endemic within companies using this approach. What impact might there be, for example, if we looked for the best that is going on and just replicated that?

8. Adopt the Right PROGRAMS:

Premise: If we bring in the latest program, whether TQM, Six Sigma, the Learning Organization, etc., and if everyone is committed to the program and cooperates to make it (the program) successful, then the program will make the company a success. So we just need to identify the best improvement program out there and adopt it.

But what if the primary result of this is that people put energy only into perfecting a program, while the company's strategy and goals fade into the background? Might that merely divert energies that should really be spent directly on improving overall business performance?

9. Introduce BEST PRACTICES:

Premise: If we get each of our most important business processes up to industry standard, then we'll achieve superior business performance. So we just need to adopt the processes that the industry leaders use to get the business results that they get.

But how do we get our people actually following those practices? And, if we're "merely" copying the best practices in the industry, won't we always be behind the leaders, who no doubt will be continuing to innovate and improve? Is this approach enough? Or is there something deeper at work that powers business improvement?

10. IMPLEMENT

Premise: Execution is the key. We'll succeed by just making it happen. Whatever it is, get out there and "Just DO it"!

But what is it that each person should do? And how is it that they should do it even better than they have been already?

Each of the above strategies is often a central part of a major turnaround strategy. By themselves, however, they may not be enough, or worse, actually distract energies from the deeper, inner shifts that need to occur in order to achieve dramatic performance gains.

The Inner and Outer Dimensions of Corporate Success

Our business culture is action oriented. Thus, companies and their leaders naturally start with a model of change and improvement that asks, "What can we *do* about this?" They focus on the actions that will solve the problem and get them the performance they want—what I call the *outer dimension*. Often missing, however, is the *inner dimension*—what goes on within people that enables them to rise to new heights and then to continue functioning there.

Best practices are actions (defined in procedures and policies that describe them) that are carried out by individuals and groups in every interaction with

Sources of Competitive Advantage

one another, with vendors, with customers, and with the community at large. They do not describe the "being" of the people who carry out those actions, how much they are motivated, disciplined, collegial, organized, or empowered. This inner dimension is a direct and necessary counterpart to (and fuel of) the outer

The INNER and OUTER Dimensions of Corporate Success

1. The OUTER Dimension

ACTION

Concerns of the OUTER Dimension - The "Hard Stuff"				
What we need to DO in order to succeed				
What Business should we be in?	**What Strategy will we use to succeed?**	**What Resources do we need?**	**What Processes/Practices shall we create & use** *(The realm of "Best Practices")*	
- Market Niches - Customer Groups - Needs to fill - Products/ Services to provide	- How to serve the market - Unique Value Proposition - Drivers of Success – and Approach on each	Resources/ Capabilities: - Financial Capital - Physical Resources - Technology - Human Resources	Marketing - to attract & retain the best cus- tomers - to grow the business	Operations - Quality - Produc- tivity - Costs
		Support Functions: Customer Service, IT, HR, etc		

2. The INNER Dimension
BEING

Concerns of the INNER Dimension - The "Soft Stuff"				
What kind of INNER QUALITIES do we need for our Company to thrive?				
Who We ARE & What we STAND for	**How We SEE the World**	**Our RELATION-SHIPS & IMPACT**	**Our MOTIVA-TION**	**Our FULFILL-MENT**
∞ Our Person-ality	∞ Seeing below the surface	∞ Respect & Caring	∞ Sense of Noble Purpose	∞ What we Care about
∞ Our Attitudes	∞ Seeing the Whole (as well as the parts)	∞ Empathy	∞ Career Goals	∞ Where we find Meaning
∞ Our Values	∞ Seeing Possibil-ities (vs. just Prob-lems)	∞ Trust	∞ Personal Growth Objectives	
∞ Our Integrity		∞ Collab-oration	∞ Discipline	
∞ Our Enthu-siasm	∞ Beliefs we hold, e.g., Believing in "our" future	What do we engender in others: - Trust? - Inspiration? - Confidence? - Collab-oration?	∞ Tenacity	

dimension described in each of the above strategies. That is, best practices require "best being" of the people working to generate superior performance.

To succeed, all companies seek to create competitive advantage. That comes not just from focus on outer sources, but also inner ones, and ultimately from the human energies that power them.

Thus, to thrive companies need to understand and focus as much on the inner dimension as they already do on the outer. The outer dimension is the delivery vehicle for the inner dimension, while the inner is the driving force behind the outer forms. The following charts detail the makeup of each dimension.

When the Inner Dimension Is Overlooked:

When the inner dimension is overlooked, it can sabotage even the best actions. Struggling companies tend to exhibit the following weak inner qualities:

1. A Focus on the Negative

Without specific attention to creating a positive culture, corporate cultures can turn negative. Some traditional improvement strategies actually engender negativity. For example, a corporate management philosophy driven by the belief that "If we can find what's wrong and fix it, then we'll have a high-performing company" causes management to walk around looking for what's wrong. People in the ranks get the message all too well: "We're not good enough," and lo and behold, they get stuck acting that way. Far from being inspired, passionate, confident, and collaborative, people become even more cynical, pessimistic, and nonproductive.

2. Limiting Beliefs

That expectations play a large role in resulting performance is well documented. If people believe a goal is unreachable, they are not likely to make a real effort to achieve it. Limiting beliefs constrain what we believe possible, what we think our people are capable of, and what our own capabilities as leaders are. So our limiting beliefs become reality.

People who believe in endless possibilities, however, are typically positive and courageous—and action-oriented. Conversely, those who believe that it's all hopeless naturally have very little motivation or commitment—and take little action.

3. Lack of Purpose

The outer-directed goal of material gain taps only a narrow level of personal motivation. When there is no purpose beyond that, most people have little desire to change, to improve, to risk, or to excel. When people have a sense of a larger, noble purpose—one that includes, for example, serving customers as whole human beings, not just consumers of their products—they are eager to learn and follow those best practices of customer service—and to invent new ones.

4. No Passion

All the best practices in the world cannot make up for people without passion about their work, their job, and their company. How can a company with low morale and a lack of passion expect to achieve great heights in performance? Yet, by focusing just on the outer actions (procedures) that people are expected to follow, without focusing on the inner meaning of those procedures, companies fail to utilize the full power of their human resources.

5. Lack of Collaboration

Companies cannot expect to succeed where employees, especially senior leaders, just carry their own individual flags. When the focus is merely on the facts, the analysis, and the decision, without focusing on the process, then collaboration often falls by the wayside. Collaboration stems from strong relationships that people form with their coworkers. It also stems from the nature of the management process created within the company.

6. Absence of Goodwill

We use outer forms—legal contracts—to make sure that each party to a contract holds to its promise. Underlying that legal form, however, can be a powerful inner dimension of goodwill. Such an underlying spirit of respect and desire for mutual benefit is a powerful inner determinant of whether that contract will be upheld or not. Without this goodwill, there is little meaningful connection between supplier and customer, let alone between the company and its employees. There is also more likelihood of friction over terms of such a contract. When market conditions change, those companies and people who have created relationships—and thus contracts—on a foundation of strong goodwill can more readily adapt and thrive.

Why the Inner Dimension Is So Important

Some people believe totally in the outer dimension. They say, "Just tell me what to do!" But they miss the essence, the very driver of stellar performance—the inner dimension. Without inner energy as the fuel, outer action often falls short even when the best practices are implemented.

CHAPTER 3

FIVE HUMAN ENERGIES THAT POWER SUCCESS

"Do you remember how electrical currents and 'unseen waves' were laughed at? The knowledge about man is still in its infancy."
—Albert Einstein

"The new leadership must be grounded in fundamentally new understandings of how the world works. The sixteenth-century Newtonian mechanical view of the universe, which still guides our thinking, has become increasingly dysfunctional in these times of increasing interdependence and change."
—Peter Senge

"Work in the invisible world at least as hard as you do in the visible."
—Jalaluddin Rumi

If the inner dimension of companies is where management can focus to generate even greater growth and profitability, then what powers that inner dimension? The answer is human energies. The management of Unitel/AT&T Canada LDS succeeded largely because they activated this hidden energy and put it to good use.

Human Energies

What do we mean by "human energies" and how do these energies power the successful corporation?

When we think about human energy, what comes to mind first is physical energy. It is the most visible form of energy, manifesting in physical exertion and movement. It certainly is what most companies cared about during the manufacturing era, with its large human physical labor component.

But physical energy is not the only energy. There is a deeper energy—in Eastern thought this is called *chi* (or *prana*)—the life force running through our bodies. Everyone possesses this life force. It is evident in physical energy, but also in mental, emotional, and spiritual energy, as well. High-producing professionals and executives expend a huge amount of this inner energy throughout the day. Though quiet, this energy can be very powerful. The energy of these people seemingly radiates from their faces.

Every corporation possesses its own energy field. You can feel it when you walk into a corporate headquarters or into any office, when you attend a meeting with people from the company, or even when you call on the phone. The energy field is created by the kinds of energy that are encouraged, which ones flow, and how they flow.

To be healthy and vibrant, a work organization must have:

- an abundance of energy available in the people of the organization;
- an ability to tap all available energy;
- free-flowing energy, unblocked by fears and/or an oppressive culture or management system;
- positive energy—focused on a clear purpose; and
- some mechanism for focusing and channeling energy to where it is needed most.

When those energies are positive, people come to work alive and fully charged, ready to dedicate their energy to their organization and to its purpose. That then translates into the willingness to do whatever it takes to get their jobs done for the benefit of customers and company alike.

Many corporations, however, are drained of the very human energies they need to succeed long term. Wilson Learning Worldwide Inc found a few years ago that "eighty percent of employees today are 'inactive' or 'just doing their jobs' and unwilling to expend their energy."[†] That's a huge amount of human potential lying dormant. Having just ten or twenty percent of employees who do not expend their energy could easily keep a company from achieving greatness.

What, then, constrains the quantity, flow, and use of energy? The positive expression of the life force within companies is stifled or distorted when:

- people are not viewed (and treated) as whole human beings;
- in particular, human spirit tends to be ignored and discouraged;
- the material and human dimensions of business have not been fully integrated; or

---

†Marjorie Kelly, "Business Ethics," *The Minneapolis Star Tribune,* March/April (1997)

• fear is rampant—within the leadership as well as the led.

Energy expended poorly can be as bad as having no energy (or more accurately, just not accessing the energy that is present). Company performance may be hampered by:

Energies out of balance: An organization that invests all of its energy in creating outer forms (such as fancy corporate offices and flashy marketing pieces) without investing in inner aspects of the company may well find itself out-performed by other companies that *do* focus on the inner energies of the company, such as its morale and employee growth.

Stuck energies: An organization may be bloated, having plenty of energy but just not using it. Or energies are easily wasted through infighting, fear, and hesitation.

Energy black holes: An organization that sucks in outside energy without creating and generating its own internal energies is essentially a black hole. We've all experienced some companies and government agencies like that. In these organizations, there is very little energy available to give out either to customers or employees.

Frenetic energy-wasters: Other organizations express lots of energy, but seemingly to no purpose other than fueling the crisis of the day.

The Five Energies That Power Successful Organizations

When we look at human energies closely, we begin to see that there are different kinds of energy available and at work. We look here at five distinct human energies. These are the primary energy sources that fuel the inner dimension of Being, and thus of participation in the work world. Each energy provides distinct qualities conducive to business excellence.

Body & Mind: The Traditional Realm of Corporate Energies

Historically, business has called primarily on just two kinds of energy—those of the Body and (more recently) those of the Mind

Energy Sources Fueling the Inner Dimension of Being

QUALITIES of Being Needed for Corporate Success				
• Effort • Stamina	• Thinking, • Analyzing • Beliefs • Decisions	• Meaning • Motivation • Enthusiasm	• Integrity • Trust • Collab- oration	• Focus • Discipline • Tenacity
ENERGY Source of these Qualities				
BODY	MIND	EMOTIONS	HEART	WILL
"Working Harder"	*"Working Smarter"*	*"Feeling"*	*"Passion"*	*"Purpose"*

Body

The first kind of energy we normally think of is the energy of *work* itself, i.e. physical effort. This is about using your "Hands" to get work done. It is the "work harder" dimension that most supervisors focus on, and it shows up in several ways:

Energy Type	Nature of the Energy	Business Manifestation
Body – Action **(The Hands)**	**Effort:** Use of physical energy to carry out work	**EXECUTION**: Producing product, delivering service, implementing programs efficiently and effectively

Be at work: Show up on time and put in a "full day's work," i.e., don't waste time on water cooler chats, long lunch hours, personal phone calls, etc. This is what has historically been meant by "work ethic."

Efficiency: Not just being at work, but producing. Efficiency is what you produce with a unit of work, measured usually either as output per

38

hour (if you are physical laborer on the production line) or output per month or year (if you are professional employee, such as a sales person). Economists call this *productivity*. In the early part of the twentieth century, management science and industrial engineering began using time and motion studies to measure human efficiency and to find ways to improve it.

Effectiveness: Beyond just being efficient: Put your energy into the most important efforts. This is what time management is all about— expending energy on the right goals, issues, and tasks. Management guru Peter Drucker put it this way: "There is nothing so useless as doing efficiently that which should not be done at all."

We use our bodies to get the work done by collecting, organizing, and then using resources to create a product or service. Despite the huge role played by technology and information in organizations, our bodies remain an essential part of work. We want people to "just get it done!" We teach time management and project planning. We develop elaborate tracking and measuring systems to see how well we are doing on this front, how much and how fast work can be accomplished.

Body energy is in part physical energy; people who are in excellent physical shape get more done than those in poor physical shape. An active, healthy physical lifestyle also helps stimulate all the other energies.

But this energy also comes from motivation.

> *A radio commercial for an accounting agency touts the work ethic of one of their temporary accountants. The boss tells the regular employee who calls in "sick" not to worry because "Bob is here." Bob, a temporary accounting worker, has already completed the year-end reports and is starting a new, important project. By the end of the phone call, the regular employee is pleading to come back in, claiming that his "head cold" is starting to clear up.*

What would most companies give to have a workforce of Bobs, people who can finish all of the work in far less time than the average employee? As the commercial suggests, the regular employee does not produce what Bob can. How, then, can we turn our company's current workforce into working dynamos like Bob?

Mind

This second form of human energy is about thinking: using the knowledge you have not only to do your job effectively, but to improve it. It's also about continually expanding your knowledge so you can be even more valuable to your employer. This is the "work smarter" dimension that more skilled supervisors focus on. It's about using your Head in productive and innovative ways.

Energy Type	Nature of the Energy	Business Manifestation
Mind – Thinking **(The Head)**	**Brain Power:** Knowledge, understanding, analysis, decision making, out-of-the-box thinking	**DECISIONS,** and decision processes, such as for business strategy, new product development, marketing programs, etc.

Mental energy manifests in:

Knowledge: about your job, your profession, and your company, including its goals, products/service, procedures, strategies and policies, customers, competition, technology, etc.

Analysis: either to develop greater insight about how to do your job even better or to address specific goals, problems, and issues;

Decision-making: to fulfill your job, to improve methods, to improve individual actions, transactions and results.

This second form of energy, mental power, has been at the frontier of business over the past two generations, with the development of such concepts as the knowledge worker, then later the learning organization, and finally more recently Intellectual Capital.

In some companies, employees are asked merely to understand—and follow—the company's procedures, no more, no less. Some organizations, however, may be willing to have employees question current processes and develop new ones. This risks upsetting "how we do things." Therefore, many companies choose to avoid this risk, thereby wasting a precious resource.

> *When I was recruited to be director of Administration for a two-hundred-person law firm, I was given an eighteen-page job description. I was expected to know and manage every detail of the firm, which is how my predecessor had handled the job. I inherited a staff of people who were used to being micromanaged. I also found that they were so overburdened with work that they hardly had time to breathe. I set out to create a strong management staff to organize the work more effectively—and to work together with them to help turn around the firm's profit slide.*

> *One of the functional managers, Terry, had been working there for many years, supervising the firm's supplies, mail and fax communications, and facilities. She came across as stoic but drained. I asked her what could be changed to improve the service and costs of her operations. As she began telling me her ideas, she became more and more animated. After getting a green light to act on these ideas, she implemented changes that resulted in substantial cost savings and service improvements.*

> *In one of our management meetings, I acknowledged the contributions that she and her people were making to the firm. To this day, her response is still etched in my memory: "I've worked here for twelve years, and nobody ever asked me for my opinion before." Here was a tremendously valuable employee (part of what we call Human Capital), whose "Hands" had been employed by the firm, but not her Head!*

> *The firm's management had previously only asked her to use her brain power to decide how to carry out their commands. Imagine how much more she could have been contributing on an ongoing basis if her management had invited her mental energy to work. How many other Terrys are out there in how many other firms, just waiting to be asked to contribute their Heads as well as their Hands?*

A survey by the Hay Group, a leading human resources firm revealed not only that fully one third of a million employees surveyed were planning to leave their current employer, but that the primary motivation for feeling that way was that their skills were not being adequately employed.

When the highest mental energies are engaged, people are able to:

• See below the surface of what is really causing various outer behaviors

- See the whole and how everything is interconnected
- See the opportunities even in the seemingly most dire situation
- Believe in and expect a positive future

We can only create what we *believe* can be created. If people are allowed to use their imaginations, to do "blue sky" thinking, to imagine what could become reality, who knows what an organization could accomplish.

Many companies do go to great lengths to create processes for tapping mental power and using it to help the company succeed, such as strategy development, scenario planning, goal setting, decision making, developing analytical methods, creating operating reports, designing systems diagrams. All these mental processes represent ways of using the mind to figure out what is going on, what should be going on, and what to do to get even better business performance. Such practices are woven into the very fabric of most companies.

These first two energies are the primary human energies that most companies see and invite to work. In today's business world, that is not enough. Some companies are finding that the energies making up human spirit are equally important.

SPIRIT

The remaining three energies together create the spirit that people bring to work.

Emotions

> *"Nothing great was ever achieved without enthusiasm."*
>
> —Ralph Waldo Emerson

The business world has long believed that emotions have no place in business—that they do not matter, and, if anything, they are an obstacle to getting things done efficiently. The very phrase "businesslike" paints a picture of business and the people involved in it as cold and devoid of any hint of emotion. There is increasing recognition, however, that this attitude is counterproductive.

> *Southwest Airlines is well known for its lighthearted flight attendants—and its profitability. Longtime (former) CEO Herb Kelleher once observed, "I've tried to create a culture of caring for people in the totality of their lives, not*

just work....Someone can go out and buy airplanes from Boeing and ticket counters, but they can't buy our culture, our esprit de corps." Southwest states, "We hire for character and attitude and then train for skills."

Kelleher is talking about something intangible, yet essential: the feelings that people have about working for Southwest Airlines.

Energy Type	Nature of the Energy	Business Manifestation
EMOTIONS - Feelings	**MEANING:** Pride, Emotional Intelligence, enthusiasm, openness, humor	**MOTIVATION**, including self-confidence, teamwork, esprit de corps

Brain power may be overrated in terms of its importance when an organization wants to create a high performance team. The emotional dimension, which enables people to feel part of a team, take pride in their accomplishments, and come to work feeling good about what they are contributing, is of equal value. Indeed, this emphasis is the cornerstone of attracting and keeping good employees and getting superior performance.

People in organizations that succeed in accessing and using emotional energies display:

• enthusiasm, like Bob from the office temp commercial
• an openness and ability to work with others
• pride in their work, company, and team
• a sense of humor and the attitude that work can and should be fun
• an ability (and responsibility) for handling negative emotions in their dealings with others.

These emotions can be powerful sources of a can-do spirit. They enable people to give their best because they *want* to, not because they feel that they *have* to. And that can make all the difference on the organization's bottom line. In a world too often filled with negative emotional energies (of fear, for example), these positive energies can pave the way for success.

When we take pride in our accomplishments, achievement becomes a reward in itself—and thus a powerful motivator. This positive emotional energy was one of the energies at work in the AT&T Canada LDS turnaround—pride in self, pride in product and service, and, equally important, pride in company.

While encouraging positive emotions, we should not lose sight of the flip side of the coin. Maintaining employees' mental health includes keeping track of when things are not going well. Emotions can of course also be negative and destructive to an organization's effectiveness. Fear can become rampant, causing companies to either ignore its threats or to study them to death rather than take action (bacause of a debilitating fear that their actions could turn out to be wrong).

Companies and individual supervisors have long used this energy to motivate—fear of loss of favor, loss of position, even loss of job—in an attempt to extract greater effort and performance. Incivility, even rage, within some employees (and supervisors) can poison the culture, causing reduced effectiveness and cooperation. Excessive ego can make everything "personal" and about "me," rather than about the customer, the company, and its purpose.

What about intuition? Decision making seems to come mostly from the head (mental energy), but often there is another kind of energy involved. Some leaders admit to a kind of "gut feel" that helps them take all the information that their Head is working on and make a decision that seems "right." Emotional energy becomes part of that process. So too does the energy of Heart.

Heart

> "Great hearts send forth steadily the secret forces that incessantly draw great events."
>
> —Ralph Waldo Emerson

The Heart has probably been the most underutilized resource available to business. The Heart can, when called on, provide important energies in achieving superior business performance that the Mind, Body, and Emotions alone cannot.

Despite the Heart's immense power, business often seems opposed to it, at least as business people perceive it. They think of the Heart as characterized by romance, valentines, soft words, chivalrous gestures, and worse, "softhearted touchy feely stuff," none of which (they say) belongs in a business setting. Instead, they value the "hard stuff," the supposed rationality of the Mind.

Yet the Heart has much to offer business. The Heart represents the capacity to care, to really care, about what one does as an employee and through being part of an organization. When people care about what they are

Energy Type	Nature of the Energy	Business Manifestation
HEART - Passion	**Values**: Integrity, courage, trust, respect, connection & unity	**PRINCIPLES**: Value-based strategies & leadership, community (from teams to strategic alliances), & service

doing, and how they do it, then they usually do it better. A company's purpose need not be about saving lives or providing food for the hungry. Employees of companies in the most mundane industries can have such a sense of commitment, such Heart energy, that they can help make it successful, in large part because of that very energy.

Heart energy is about values. It is about a sense of community and mutual respect. It also is about collaboration and service. Leaders who recognize the value of Heart energy and call forth these energies in themselves and in their organizations tend to be more effective in creating true teamwork, where people trust and respect each other and honor the whole person. More than that, they use Heart energies to build a truly customer-oriented service organization. Such companies achieve stronger business performance as a result.

When Heart energies are welcomed and expressed, they manifest as:

Passion: about the work and its purpose. How many people leave this at home? Yet it can make all the difference in making work more than just a job and a company more than just a place to work;

Integrity: expressed consistently through ethical behavior and honesty. This is the source of values-based leadership;

Courage: to take action when others are afraid to move forward and to stand firm on principles when others would compromise;

Trust and faith: in colleagues and in the ultimate success of the enterprise. Expecting success helps beget success.

> **Caring and service to others:** This is the source of Servant Leadership, in which the leader leads by serving others—an approach made popular by Robert Greenleaf and other authors over the last several decades, which ultimately traces its origins back several millennium to spiritual leaders in the East and West.

> **Unity and interconnection:** so people can collaborate—even with adversaries—because they are able to see and act from their connection and common values, rather than from their separation.

What about love?

Heart, of course, is also about love. The problem with talking about love is that it's easy to get sidetracked on romantic love. The Greeks use separate words for romantic love (*eros*) and brotherly love (*filios*). Brotherly love permeates those heart qualities listed above and contributes to a vibrant, successful company.

Heart is beginning to take its rightful place at the corporate table. And with Heart starting to be recognized as an important energy source for successful companies, we can expect that those companies that thrive will indeed be a place of love. That kind of Heart energy was clearly evident in the lobby of that Toronto office building the day that the employees of AT&T Canada LDS said goodbye to their CEO.

Will

"Strength does not come from physical capacity. It comes from an indomitable will."
—Mahatma Gandhi

"The moment one definitely commits oneself, then Providence moves too. All sorts of things occur to help one that would never have otherwise occurred … unforeseen incidents and meetings and material assistance, which no man could have dreamed would have come his way."
—Goethe

"Always bear in mind that your own resolution to succeed is more important than any one thing."
—Abraham Lincoln

"We can do anything we want, if we stick to it long enough."
—Helen Keller

If the Heart is the most underappreciated resource, then Will is the most misused and mistrusted. Why? Because it is often ego-centered: "My Will over your will" kind of behavior. Many people experience Will—especially in the work place—as negative, the absence of freedom, as being under the thumb of someone else, most often the boss or the company.

Energy Type	Nature of the Energy	Business Manifestation
WILL – Purpose	**COMMITMENT:** to serving both individual and company purpose	**PURPOSEFUL ACTION**, with focus, discipline, and organizational alignment

But Will energy, when directed to the highest purpose of the company or the greatest good in any situation, is crucial to companies' success. When Will energies focus on what is best for everyone involved, not just the individual, but also the company and all its stakeholders, it becomes a powerful and necessary energy for building a vibrant, effective organization.

In fact, without positive Will energies, a company is like a ship without a rudder. The ship may have all kinds of wonderful attributes, but it is just drifting in the water, with neither a clear direction nor forward movement.

When Will energy is expressed positively, it manifests as:

- High and strong purpose in what the organization stands for, why it is in business, and what difference it is supposed to make;
- Focus—concentrating energies on the most important priorities;
- Discipline—staying on target and moving forward;

Will energy also is about the people in an organization. What is the highest purpose for each person? While each individual is responsible for figuring this out, companies with healthy Will energy can provide an environment where people freely explore what their own highest purpose is, how it relates to the company's highest purpose, and how their job can lead to individual and organizational congruence and mutual support. As a source of motivation, such exploration adds an important dimension beyond that of using one's skills and experience merely to earn a financial return.

What about power?

Some leaders use personal power to exert dominion over their staff. This is a negative manifestation of Will. Whether it stems from the leader's ego or from fear, it results in a kind of micromanagement that usually saps other peoples' energy, stifles initiative, and ultimately crushes creativity. Some people express this kind of will power often just to show that they can exert their own personal power. Others engage in a battle of wills that ends up being about the individuals involved rather than about the good of the organization.

Over the past several decades, more empowering and inspiring ways to lead have emerged than merely exerting one's personal power over others to "force" them to perform. Servant Leadership is one such model.

When companies tap into the higher purpose of Will, then Heart energy is unleashed, which in turn calls forth the other energies. This happens often through a clear vision and mission that is about the highest good for the company, its customers, and its employees. It also happens in small, seemingly insignificant individual moments and events. The joining of purpose (expressed through Will), passion (expressed through Heart), and meaning (experienced through the Emotions) combine to make for a powerful and focused release of Human Spirit—all dedicated to both the company's and the individuals' growth and prosperity.

A Fully Energized Company

An energized company invites people to bring all of themselves to work. It recognizes not only the importance of Mind and Body (thought and action) but also Spirit (Emotions, Heart, and Will). These energies flow through the human relationships within the company and with key partners outside the company. Leaders in energized enterprises draw forth these energies and utilize them to serve the company's mission, to live its values, and to achieve sustainable growth and prosperity.

Part II tells the story of the revitalization of Unitel/AT&T Canada LDS, focusing on what was *done*, but also on the *energy* with which it was done. You will see what CEO Bill Catucci and his team did. You will see verifiable measures of the company's success—quality levels, customer retention, employee morale, and shareholder value.

As you read about the actions that Bill and his team took, however, think not just in terms of "best practices" but also about the underlying energies that powered those actions, and the impact of those energies on employees, on customers, on vendors, and on the bottom line.

In these chapters, you will see wonderful forms that the people of AT&T Canada LDS created that marked great advances in their business performance. But the marvel to them and to the people they touched were not so much the forms, but the energy behind those forms.

So, in the story you will see in Part II, look with "new eyes," not just at the outer forms of corporate revitalization, but also at the underlying energy of Human Spirit.

PART II

REVITALIZING A
NEAR-DEATH COMPANY

CHAPTER 4

(HOW) CAN THIS COMPANY BE SAVED?

Unitel, a Canadian telecommunications company with 2600 employees and one billion dollars in assets, was fast approaching what many expected would be its end. With nearly $700 million in debt, lagging sales, and high costs, it was losing $1 million a day during 1995.

Only a few years earlier, Unitel had begun with great promise and great resources. Canadian Pacific Railway and Rogers Communications had created the company to compete in the telecommunications industry. Several large banks—the Bank of Nova Scotia, the Royal Bank of Canada, and Toronto Dominion—had provided financing. AT&T had taken a minority position in the company.

By early 1995, Unitel's cash flow problems were affecting its overall business. Needed capital investment was postponed. Quality declined. Its market share, which was 9.2 percent for business customers and 4.5 percent for residential customers, produced revenues too low to cover its high fixed costs.

The CEO office had become a revolving door as the company's owners scrambled to bring in new leadership to try to stem the losses and create positive cash flow. Meanwhile, a steady stream of customers and top employees left the company.

The founding companies of Unitel sought to restructure their ownership, but none of the owners was willing to buy out the others. Everyone knew that Unitel's demise would have a rippling negative effect throughout the Canadian economy: Canada's efforts to introduce competition in the long-distance telephone market would be frustrated, and those institutions with major financial stakes in Unitel would suffer considerable losses. For Unitel's 43,000 business customers and 342,000 residential customers to switch providers would be time consuming and problematic. Many suppliers would likely get paid no more than ten cents on the dollar.

Finally, Unitel's employees would likely be out on the street.

The banks decided to put Unitel up for sale to recover whatever they could from the debt they held in the company. They hoped that a buyer would step forward, thereby avoiding the inevitable economic pain that a dissolution of Unitel would cause. With their fiduciary responsibility, they had put the wheels in motion, even if there *was* no apparent buyer.

Andy Kent, lawyer for the Royal Bank of Canada, prepared a search for a partner or acquirer for Unitel. This was a situation with a myriad of challenges making it far more complex than other deals in which he had participated. Mentally, he created the checklist of challenges:

> The company had already suffered from the fact that the shareholders were not of one mind. By mid-1995, the shareholder group had fallen out, with no consensus on strategy. The company was adrift, with no unified direction from the top.

> The company was losing cash at an alarming rate. The banks and the shareholders were all unwilling to provide additional resources.

> AT&T, a likely candidate to invest in the company, had been slow to express interest in even bidding. Other possible buyers would likely offer a fraction of the value of the banks' debt in Unitel.

> Without an equity sponsor, there was no future for Unitel.

Clearly, some kind of governance was needed, even during the search for an acquiring company. The banks chose a five-person independent committee to bring proper guidance in the interim.

Andy saw that any deal would be extremely difficult to reach, not only because of the company's dire financial state, but also because there were so many stakeholders involved: the ownership group of companies, which included several smaller ones as well as Canadian Pacific Railway, Rogers Communications, and AT&T; plus several banks, each with its own agenda.

AT&T Decides to Look at Unitel

AT&T's twenty percent share in Unitel stemmed from its desire to participate in the Canadian telecommunications market. In order to serve international markets, and especially business customers with overseas divisions, telecommunications companies needed facilities in major countries so they could provide seamless service for their customers making international calls. Without such facilities, they had to secure capacity from other companies. Owning facilities in Canada would allow AT&T to serve its existing customer base more cost effectively. It would also improve the quality of the Canadian network.

At the time, AT&T's goal was to have fifty percent of AT&T's business generated from international markets by the year 2000. In this respect, the alliance with Unitel was crucial. One hundred and twenty-five of the top three hundred U.S. firms had branch offices in Canada. AT&T had to provide these customers with seamless telecommunications service or it would be unable to compete globally.

With Unitel failing and on the auction block, AT&T had to rethink its entire Canadian strategy. So the company tapped Bill Catucci, a thirty-three-year AT&T veteran, to lead its effort to decide whether to make a bid for Unitel, and if so, what kind of a deal to propose.

Bill had led several other integrated teams that looked at serious problems and big opportunities. His tax law experience, extensive AT&T lobbying experience, and earlier sales and marketing experience provided a good background. Perhaps just as important, Bill enjoyed the challenge of finding and implementing solutions to complex issues. He liked breaking out of conventional thinking to look at tough challenges with fresh perspectives. He saw himself as a contrarian. When conventional wisdom argued there was no solution, he became even more passionate about finding one.

The challenge was to put a plan together quickly—one that would turn Unitel around and be satisfactory to AT&T and to the banks. And it had to beat out any competing offers.

Time was short. They were starting late in the banks' process of soliciting offers.

The first step for Bill was to put together his Unitel Deal Team. Getting outside consultants to provide marketing, network, and finance expertise was relatively easy. Within AT&T, however, it was no easy task to find experienced people who would devote their time to such an effort. Everyone already had jobs, and this was going to be a full-time project. The best people were the busiest, and the people Bill wanted worked for other executives, so he couldn't simply command them to join his team. They had to be drawn into this important challenge, just as Bill was. And, with the time pressures they were up against, Bill had to have their assurances that they would be there when he needed them and complete their work on time.

Bill enlisted Karen Jeisi, a longtime AT&T employee, to be the project leader. Karen had worked with Bill on a prior assignment and had already been involved with Unitel for AT&T. She and Bill identified the people they wanted on the team.

The team eventually was made up of AT&T people with experience in telecommunications networks and technology, finance, marketing, and strategy, plus attorneys with tax expertise. It also included consultants from Monitor Group, an external strategy consulting firm, and Morgan Stanley, an investment banking firm.

Developing a Plan to Save Unitel

When the team assembled in a conference room at AT&T's Basking Ridge, New Jersey, headquarters in July of 1995 for its first meeting, many had reservations about the prospects for Unitel. Some team members were already knowledgeable about Unitel—and its problems. They wondered, *Was Unitel even a viable business?* They knew there had been so many different strategies that a kind of schizophrenia had set in that seemed to leave the company dead in the water. Should they be in the major markets or in the mid market? Should they go after cost cuts or build for growth?

Larry Hudson, AT&T's network expert and a member of the Deal Team, knew Unitel's network firsthand. He told the group, "Unitel's competitor doesn't have the embedded costs that Unitel does because they built their network from scratch. They used the latest technology. They only built what they needed. They didn't try to serve everybody. Unitel had a network sitting there already that Canadian Pacific Railway had built over the years. So those costs are just sitting there."

That wasn't the end of the bad news. "The network is also far too big and therefore too expensive. This is partially from uneven investment in the network infrastructure. For example, they installed a $20 million switching machine that has much larger capacity than they need. So all those costs just sit there and are spread across a relatively small volume of calls. Unitel has a fill factor of only five percent. Until you get the fill factor up to around eighty percent, your costs are going to eat you alive."

"Not only is it an expensive network, it's not a very good network. The technology is just too old. How can you expect to compete with the big guys when your network isn't good enough to provide the variety and the quality of services you need to attract and keep good customers?"

The team looked at other aspects of Unitel's current business: quality and service issues, sales and organizational issues, and debt servicing issues.

In the meantime, they investigated what was wrong from customers' perspectives. Typical customer reactions to Unitel included:

> *"Their service is not good enough. There are calling errors. The system goes down frequently."*

> *"Unitel is not providing the kinds of services that their competitors are providing. So no wonder they are having trouble holding onto customers."*

> *"I hate to do that (leave), because I hate to see only two competitors. And Call-Net doesn't even try to serve the large corporate customer. That leaves only Stentor. Unitel started out by trying to provide services tailored to our kind of company, but I think they lost interest. Or maybe they're so busy fighting their own fires that they don't have the energy to focus on the customer."*

> *"They seem to be cutting back on going after the large customer market. They talk a lot about operational excellence, but they don't deliver it. How can they expect to compete with the big guy on his own strategy, costs and quality?*

It was not immediately clear what Unitel's current business model was or what markets they were concentrating on—the residential or the corporate. The company had entered the long-distance market with a focus on large customers—the business market—but recently had been losing market share there.

The Deal Team developed and considered several alternative strategies. Morgan Stanley, the investment bank on the Deal Team, argued for a **full-service strategy**. They felt that only if the company provided a full range of telecommunications products and services—local, long-distance, wireless, and Internet—would it succeed.

A second option—**operational excellence combined with low cost**—was not economically feasible due to Unitel's relatively small size.

Instead, they decided that Unitel's overall strategy should be to develop the capability to **deliver superior service and to provide customized services for large customers for long-distance service**. The company would also strive to gain market share through **high-touch customer service.**

The resulting business plan for Unitel called for upgrading the network, growing revenues, and reducing operating losses by fifty percent the first year and steadily thereafter, so that by year three the company would begin turning a profit. The team figured that with another $250 million investment, Unitel could be saved—and could develop a profitable business.

New Ownership

Next was the challenge of selling the plan to AT&T and to the banks. Both parties wanted Unitel to succeed, but neither was looking to come up with the money.

Bill presented the plan to the AT&T management group in late August. They approved of the business strategy and projected financials for a revamped Unitel. The question of who would come up with the $250 million was left unanswered, as was the question of who would be the new owners.

Bill and the team needed to figure out how to cash out the existing ownership and deal with both the banks and AT&T in a way that everybody would accept—and that would attract the funding that Unitel needed.

Where would the money come from and who would be owners besides AT&T?

Bill figured that AT&T's competition for purchasing Unitel was Call-Net. Its proposal was likely to be a "bare-bones" offer to buy Unitel at a fraction of the value of the banks' outstanding loans.

By contrast, the much more integrated and holistic proposal conceived by Bill and his team might be much more attractive because all stakeholders had a chance of coming away winners. If the banks walked away from the company, Bill reckoned the union would be angry, the employees would suffer, the community would be upset, and the industry would be hurt.

Such a holistic approach, however, would also be complicated. A problem or slip-up in any one aspect could kill it.

Bill and two members of his team met with the three bank-appointed board members of Unitel plus their investment bankers and lawyers. In his presentation, Bill avoided phrases like "This is our last and final offer" but also conveyed that AT&T was a serious participant. He explained that if the proposal he put on the table was unsatisfactory, then AT&T was willing to discuss and search for an appropriate resolution. He conveyed confidence that he and his team could deliver the goods.

Recognizing the importance of making Unitel a viable competitor, Bill emphasized how AT&T's proposal would be good for the industry and competition. He explained that AT&T's leadership of Unitel would bring considerable innovation to the industry and that they could attract customers that the competition could not.

Bill wanted to get everyone looking at the same problem and trying to come up with a reasonable solution for both sides. He wanted everyone to come away saying, "We're going to make this company work together." After all, "these people are going to be on the new Unitel board."

Andy Kent (the lead bank's lawyer) commented later that the discussions reflected the growth of an "unconditional positive regard" for one another. Instead of merely fine tuning their points of view and engaging in hard negotiations, the participants took time to learn more about the other side's issues, constraints, problems, and goals. When all else fails, reflected Andy, "kindness is a great strategy."

The more the Deal Team worked together, the more the team members felt as if they were working for *Unitel*—not just solely as representatives of AT&T. The team saw its job as building a partnership among AT&T and the banks in order to save the company.

Eventually, the funding and ownership issues were successfully negotiated. The banks, which stood to lose most or all of the $900 million debt they held in the company, agreed to reduce that amount by $100 million. They also agreed to invest $125 million in additional capital. In return, they would own sixty-seven percent[†] of the company. The founding companies, Canadian Pacific and Rogers Communications, would be cashed out. AT&T would contribute its technology, its brand name, and $125 million in additional capital. In return, it would own thirty-three percent of Unitel.

After further negotiation, AT&T agreed to allow Unitel to change its name to AT&T Canada Long Distance Services once Unitel's quality was sufficiently upgraded.

When the deal was announced, the papers rang out with the news that Unitel had been saved. There was much rejoicing. All that was needed now was to find a new CEO who would lead the company back from the depths.

Despite his recommending several possible CEOs for Unitel to the banks, Bill Catucci, after retiring from AT&T, became Unitel's fourth CEO on January 8, 1996.

---

†28% for Bank of Nova Scotia, 23% for Toronto Dominion, and 16% for Royal Bank

CHAPTER 5

SHARED VISION AND VALUES

K en Sackley, Unitel's sales manager for the province of Alberta, had been a Unitel employee from the creation of the company four years earlier and had worked for Canadian Pacific before Unitel existed. He was well aware of Unitel's financial troubles.

Ken had seen the arrival and departure of senior executives back at headquarters. In Calgary, several time zones west of the Toronto headquarters, Ken and his group were cushioned from the problems at headquarters. In fact, his group prided itself on its independence and good performance despite the company's problems. People in the group liked each other and worked well together.

One of Ken's roles was to function as a link with the head office. Calling Toronto for resources or guidance was never an easy experience: calls frequently went unreturned, and people he needed to contact had often left their jobs without letting him know. So Ken was relieved to hear that the company had new ownership and new financial capital. When he heard that the new CEO was yet another executive sent from AT&T, he rolled his eyes. His impression of CEOs in general was not great. His view of American ones was of men who had the answers and just wanted to impose their approaches on the organization without really listening to the people who were out in the field making things happen.

Ken was thus surprised and interested to learn that on his first day at Unitel, the new CEO planned to show up at the annual sales conference (January 8, 1996). When Ken looked around at the start of the sales conference, the new CEO was not there. Eventually someone got up and said, "Bill Catucci is coming, but he's going to be a little late."

Ken wondered, *What does that mean? Since it is the CEO's first day, maybe higher-level meetings are preventing him from attending?*

Finally, that afternoon, their new CEO arrived. Bill went directly to the front of the room. The meeting immediately gave way to him. Bill turned to face the sales people, and said, "I apologize for being late."

Ken could hardly believe his ears. *This is a CEO apologizing to us? That's refreshing! We're actually getting a CEO who's going to apologize once in a while! Most don't. This guy is basically saying that we are important and that he's going to treat us with respect.*

Bill explained that he had tried to fly out of New York City, but the airport was shut down because of a snowstorm. So, as he put it, "I just hopped in my car and drove to Toronto."

Ken's jaw dropped. *This guy drove hundreds of miles through a snowstorm just to meet with us today? None of us would have driven through upstate New York and Ontario. We would have stayed home and called in to say, "See you tomorrow."* Even then, Ken realized what a powerful message Bill was sending: that everyone was important, and that when you've made a commitment, you keep it.

Bill told them he had taken the job because he believed that the company deserved to succeed for the employees, the customers, the shareholders, and even the country. He pledged to do everything he could to turn the company around and asked for their help and involvement in that task. After he spoke, and before they resumed their agenda, Ken and several others went up to him to introduce themselves and welcome him.

Not everyone was encouraged. Bill was the fourth CEO in five years. It was hard to see how he was going to turn the company around, with or without their help.

Ken, however, believed Bill from the start. He was excited about what the immediate future held and looked forward to Bill being the one CEO who might actually succeed.

Back at his office in Calgary, Ken told people about Bill and the word spread quickly throughout the company that the new CEO had *driven through a snowstorm* "just" to show up at a sales conference.

A New Vision & Mission Fueled by the CEO's Passion

Bill saw his role as first a strategic one. He had to shape the strategy chosen by the Deal Team in a way that recognized the company's existing and planned strengths as well as the realities of the marketplace. And it needed to be a strategy for which he could get buy-in from his people and that they could implement.

The company was, at the time, acting on Bill's *predecessor's* strategic path. The former CEO's strategy said: in order to compete in the market place, the company has to cut costs, lower prices, and get out of those products and services that might be high cost (yet, ironically, also high value).

The strategy that Bill and his AT&T Deal Team had developed as part of the restructuring of Unitel was to focus on business customers, offering them high quality and customized service. This represented a major shift in direction for the organization. He knew it would not happen overnight.

Moreover, the organization was in disarray. Only one of the senior executives remained, and much of the rest of the organization had left. So rebuilding the organization would also be a must—not just in terms of filling empty positions, but in terms of restoring an organizational pulse.

Bill started by developing a brief, compelling vision for Unitel, the downtrodden and underperforming company he had taken the reins of.

The Vision of a New Unitel: To become the premier long-distance company in Canada.

Along with this high vision, he created a specific mission that would guide the company's strategy development and implementation—and inspire the organization to achieve the new vision for Unitel. He had not found one from prior management. Believing that a powerful mission statement could be a powerful tool in leading the company, he created this mission:

Unitel's New Mission Statement

The company would:

1. Deliver superior products and services to customers over the highest quality network at competitive prices,
2. Become one of the finest companies to work for in Canada by providing a work environment where employees can achieve their best,
3. Provide good returns to shareholders, and
4. Contribute positively to the communities in which employees live and work.

Selling the Company's New Vision and Mission

Part of the power of any vision and mission is its transparency. People needed to know about the new mission. Bill began articulating and sharing the vision at every meeting with employees. It was published in every issue of the company newsletter, along with periodic updates on what the company was doing to achieve the mission.

Creating the vision is only one step; anyone can create a fancy vision statement. Bill knew he also had to validate it. It would only work if people bought into it, if they were willing to work toward it. So he met with employees in Toronto in a large auditorium first so they could get to know him and second so he could share his vision for the company and its mission.

The employees were naturally skeptical and cynical—just what one would expect from a group of people who had been through the turmoil of Unitel's troubles. He understood their skepticism and acknowledged it.

Bill also met with smaller groups of employees, described his commitment to the company, and began sharing his vision for the company. The employees shot back their own questions: "Well, how long are you going to stay?" "What's the most important thing you're going to do here?" "What do you think about the network?" He answered the questions he could and told them when he did not know the answer.

Gradually, during these meetings Bill was able to focus more on the vision and less on the fears and concerns of the employees. The more he shared the vision, the more he realized that he was getting a positive reaction to the vision. These sharings began to take on the aura of a religious revival meeting. Bill believed in the vision. He had passion for it and he shared that passion. He joyfully took on the task of selling people and aligning them around the vision. He worked at being consistent about it, not only believing in it, but also being honest about it.

Values from the Heart of the Company

Bill then turned his attention to values. It would be easy for him to define the values himself for the company. But he believed that was not good enough. He decided he wanted to put the question to the employees themselves.

Some people say that the CEO should write the values. But Bill reasoned: *I've got 2600 people in this organization. Do I trust them or not? Are they going to come up with values like "we all ought to make a lot more money"?*

Bill believed he had to lead the effort—emphasize its importance, encourage participation, inspire contributions—but not write the values himself. So he opted for trust and asked several individuals to go out to the far reaches of the company in order to learn what people wanted the company's values to be. He was confident that the values they would come up with would be no different from the values he would create himself.

Unitel had been a company bleeding red ink profusely, where the primary concern had been to cut costs. Yet here was the new CEO asking employees what they wanted their company to *stand for*. Focus groups met throughout Canada. People shared their feelings with each other and contributed to the development of the company's values.

The answer came back that employees wanted a company that values:

• Integrity

• Respect for people

• Customer service

• Teamwork

Bill wrote to all the employees. "Here are the values that you all think we ought to have. We agree. Thus, these are now our company's values." He later added Prudent Risk-Taking.

Embedding Values into a Company's Fabric

Once the values were established, Bill wanted to do more than just print placards proclaiming them. He wanted to embed the values in actions, starting with his own. Every time he talked with employees, he made sure that he reiterated the values and how important they were to him and to the company. He wanted them to know that he did not intend to sacrifice the values to some other goal.

People asked, "What's the most important value?"

Bill's answer was swift and simple. "Integrity. If you don't have integrity, you're not going to have the rest. If you're not honest, if you don't meet commitments, if you don't keep your word, you're not going to be successful, and we have to do that. And I will tell you this: we have a problem in this company with integrity. We have a problem, internally and externally. The press has painted us with a reputation that is less than honest."

"We can never, never let that happen again. There are certain things that are not gray. They have to be black or white, and that's one of them. I want every single employee of this company to get up in the morning, look in the mirror, and say, 'I'm honest. I want to work for an honest company. We do not do anything that's wrong, even if it helps our bottom line.'"

Talk is cheap. Employees waited to see what would happen when push came to shove. Bill looked for situations in which to demonstrate the importance of these values and their power and ways to send a message.

The Vancouver Switching Station Goes Down

Within his first few weeks on the job, Bill received a phone call from an engineer in Vancouver. "We have a major problem—the switching machines have seized up, and we're not able to provide service." Thousands of Unitel customers were without long distance service because a surge in calls caused the switching station to fail.

Before the restructuring, the $500,000 required to expand capacity and upgrade the network was not available—or had been used to make debt payments. When overloaded with call volume, the switching machines had failed.

Customers barraged Unitel with frantic calls. They called their sales reps, the customer service people, anyone they could reach in the company. Some were experiencing lost sales. Sales reps had no answers to their questions. Customers threatened to leave—and to sue.

The network people had nobody to call. The network operations officer had left the company, and there was no COO. The engineer asked for Bill's help. The challenge was not only to restore service but to restore confidence.

At times like this, employees and customers find out who the CEO really is. People want to see how the CEO reacts in a crisis. Does he crumble? Does he hide? Who is he under pressure? The pressure was definitely on.

Bill's attitude had always been, *Let's take something that looks really bad and throw a curve ball at it and turn it into something good. People might think, "This guy's sort of Pollyanna—a little wacko."* But Bill knew well that there are lots of seemingly bad situations that you can turn to your advantage. He believed *this* could be one of them.

First, he was not going to go the recriminations or finger-pointing route. He wanted to set a different model than what was expected in a company in this kind of condition, where "shoot the messenger" was probably what people would expect. Instead, he quickly convened a meeting of Unitel senior staff responsible for network engineering, operations, sales, customer service, and finance.. He held the meeting in the main boardroom to send a message.

Jumping past the question of how it happened, Bill focused immediately on the question of what could be done about it. The first challenge was to get Northern Telecom, their software company, to create a fix and do it fast. This would get the network working again and expand its capacity. The finance people wanted to know how much it would cost. Bill responded, "This is not so much a cost issue as it is a survival issue. We can't *not* do this." They quickly negotiated the price and the technical solution was set in motion.

Meanwhile, Bill asked this senior staff group to go off and think about ways in which they could turn the situation to their advantage. People were surprised.

Later, when they returned, he explained further, "What a fabulous opportunity we have here! Customers are upset. Sales reps are worried. And to think that we can turn this into a great situation for us! How? Simple. We're not going to hide. We're going to take responsibility and fix this thing."

He told the group that he wanted to send a letter to customers explaining the situation. "In this letter, we're going to take responsibility for this failure and tell them what we are doing about it. We're going to show them that this is never going to happen again—that we are a company that makes commitments and keeps them." He invited their contributions to the letter and added that it would come directly from him, the CEO. In fact, he would write it himself with their input.

In the letter, Bill was candid and open. He talked about how his years in business had taught him the importance of quality and customer service. He committed to providing that kind of quality to them in the future and promised that never again would the system be shut down due to lack of capacity.

The letters went out immediately. The sales people received letters too, with a message to go to customers and tell the story.

The sales people were encouraged for a change—even in such a dire situation. *"Now I can go up to my customer and say, 'Look, here's our CEO saying this'!"*

They followed up with calls to selected customers, setting up visits to many companies by Bill and a team of sales representatives, customer service people, and network technicians. All employees were apprised of the situation in a letter from Bill.

How easy it would have been for the new CEO to hide, waiting for better times to show his face in the marketplace! But Bill saw this as an opportunity to meet the heads of his customers face-to-face and establish a personal relationship with them. The power of corporate truth, responsibility, and commitment—expressed through the presence of the CEO—helped to stem the tide of departing customers and to begin turning around employee morale.

Investing in Human Capital: Sending a Check and a Message

Before even becoming CEO, Bill had reviewed an employee survey conducted for the company by the Hay Group, a human resource consulting firm. He had imagined that morale was low but had no idea just how low it actually was. Unitel ranked near the bottom of five hundred North American companies tracked in the Hay Group survey. When he discovered this, he resolved that this would become an important dimension of the leadership of the company.

He also was apprised of a budget for executive bonuses. Without the performance to warrant payment of these bonuses, let alone the executives to reward (most top positions were empty), Bill could have just put these funds back into the hopper. Instead, he began to wonder how he could use the funds creatively to send another message. He decided to divide the bonus budget by the number of total employees and send each one a check. The amount was only $175, and people close to him advised against the move. "We're not even profitable. We need the money for investment in the company. Plus, it's a pittance. People will be insulted."

Bill responded, "I think we ought to make this investment, no matter how small, in the people of the company." He sent a personal letter to every employee. In part, it said, "This is a small amount. But I want you to have it as a token of what we can accomplish together in making this company the best it can be." Bill made sure he sent it to their homes so that each employee would likely open it in front of his or her family.

Within days, Bill began receiving letters from employees—and their spouses—filled with appreciation for the gesture and the money, along with personal comments of appreciation, such as, "We have not even been able to go out for a meal in months." People thanked their new CEO and pledged their support to the company.

CHAPTER 6

LEADERSHIP PRESENCE

B ill inherited an executive organization with no people in it. The organizational structure had seven top jobs, but nearly everyone had left. There were no business unit heads, no chief operating officer, and no chief financial officer.

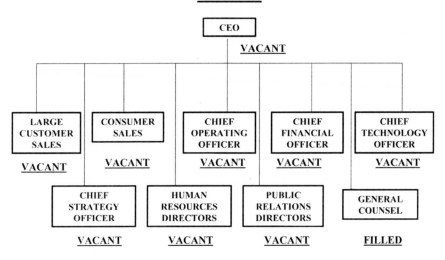

Unitel Organization Chart
12-31-95

CEO
VACANT

LARGE CUSTOMER SALES	CONSUMER SALES	CHIEF OPERATING OFFICER	CHIEF FINANCIAL OFFICER	CHIEF TECHNOLOGY OFFICER
VACANT	VACANT	VACANT	VACANT	VACANT

CHIEF STRATEGY OFFICER	HUMAN RESOURCES DIRECTORS	PUBLIC RELATIONS DIRECTORS	GENERAL COUNSEL
VACANT	VACANT	VACANT	FILLED

Unitel was perceived as a dead company. Bill recognized that it would not be enough merely to say to potential recruits that the company had been restructured and infused with more financial capital. He knew he had to present a compelling vision for them, align them with it, and get them excited and motivated.

The banks and people within Unitel expected, but also feared, that the new CEO would bring up Americans to fill the empty positions. Bill vowed not to do that. Instead, he looked for talent within the company, sharing his vision for the company with those whom he wanted to take leadership roles in bringing that vision to fruition.

It took Bill about four months to fill the seven open positions. The COO was the one person whom Bill did bring up from AT&T in the States.

The others were Unitel employees, including George Harvey, a prior CEO and experienced person who was not being utilized. Bill received advice to ask George to leave the company. But Bill saw strength in George's understanding of the business, his relationship with customers, and his mental and physical toughness. He saw a no-nonsense attitude.

But how does the new CEO invite a former CEO to become "merely" a business unit head, a man who had reported to Boards of Directors for the past seventeen years? Bill met with George and described his vision for Unitel, the importance of the Commercial Services Business unit, and the need to have someone of George's caliber lead it. He then asked George if he would like to be that business head, and George responded with enthusiasm. Bill knew the key to a healthy relationship would be to respect George and his talents and just let him do his thing.

Connecting with Employees

Even while building his top management team, Bill felt the urge to connect personally with Unitel employees. The Hay Group Employee Survey had shown that the employees had low opinions of their management and the direction of their company. A first step, even before fixing all that was wrong with the company, would be to go out and meet the people of Unitel.

Bill set out to visit Unitel offices spread across the vast Canadian country. His assistant called to set up a visit to Calgary. Ken Sackley, the sales manager who met Bill at the sales conference on Bill's first day, naturally expected that Bill would like to have a few meetings set up with customers and perhaps receive a formal presentation. But Bill's assistant said, "No, he just wants to spend the day in your office." Puzzled, Ken asked, "What does he want to *do*?" The answer: "He wants to get to know everybody."

Bill called Ken and added, "Don't plan any appointments. I just want to be in your office. Is that okay?"

"Okay," Ken responded, as he tried to grasp what was going on. *The CEO is asking my permission?*

Sure enough, the first time that Bill visited Calgary, he spent the whole day in the office with no meetings, nothing scheduled. He just wandered around saying hello to people. He sat down in people's cubicles. After some friendly banter, he would ask, "What are you working on?" Each person would get a few minutes to describe what he or she was doing. In almost every case, Bill offered some kind of insight or encouragement to keep going.

Later, as Ken listened to the excited feedback from his staff, he could feel the difference. Bill's message to people boiled down to: "I need you to do this and to be successful. You can make the decisions needed. You don't need anybody to tell you. You do the right thing."

"Sure, the company adopted a set of values," Ken observed later, "but we really learned to understand Bill's values through his visits. He valued every individual—plain and simple." On a later visit to Alberta, Bill asked to visit the operations group. Ken reflected, *No CEO has ever asked to visit the operations group.* Bill struck up a conversation with a technician, an older man who had served in the military. They shared stories of Army life, and every time Bill visited Alberta, he called the employee up to say hello.

At the end of Bill's first visit, Ken drove him back to the airport. Ken was used to this kind of ride. You try to do a debrief: How was your visit and all that. On this ride, however, Ken could not even get a word in edgewise. Bill talked enthusiastically the whole way, about the operation, about what Ken was doing, and described how impressed he was with the people. "Ken, you have a great team here." Ken began to feel like a genius. Most executives are quick to focus on the negative in some instinctual attempt to eliminate mistakes and problems. Bill focused instead on the positive and the potential, and seemed even to exaggerate the good.

As they said goodbye at the airport, Bill took Ken's hand firmly and grasped his arm with his other hand. Bill looked him in the eye and said, "Ken, what I need you to do is to lead us here. I need you to do everything you can to make our company the best it can be. I'm counting on you." He did not wait for a reply. He did not ask for a commitment. He just turned and left.

Driving back from the airport, Ken felt his heart in his throat. Never before had he felt so empowered or so uplifted by anybody. He knew that there was no way he would let Bill down; the surge of willpower he experienced made him feel unstoppable.

This scene was repeated throughout Canada, one Unitel location at a time, one group at a time, one person at a time.

It was important to Bill to connect with people. He told his executive assistant to allow time in his schedule for people to drop in and for him to wander around. Later, he observed, "I used to walk around the building just to see what was happening. I'd have coffee, eat pastry, and talk to people. I'd know their names. I'd know their nickname or a little about their family. I'd just breeze through. Sometimes I'd do it at a time when something good was happening, and I'd tell them about it. It was a way of communicating. They're right in the building. I'd see them down in the food court or outside."

He showed up when people least expected it. Every once in awhile, particularly on Sundays, Bill would go downtown to the telemarketing center. He also did this in other parts of the country. He would call up a sales person and say, "Hey, I happen to be here. How 'bout having a little soda?" He wanted to go where they didn't expect him. In many cases, people said, "We had never seen the CEO before. We didn't even know who he was. And now we see that he's no different from anybody else. He just happens to have this job."

Bill wanted people to approach *him* as well. When the Edmunston, New Brunswick, call center had its official opening, Charlotte Daigle-Basque, its leader, was thrilled that the CEO took the time to come and participate in the opening celebration. Before leaving, he said to Charlotte, "I'm so impressed with your team, would you please make sure that when you come to Toronto you give me a call so we can meet and you can tell me how the team is doing?"

Charlotte's immediate thought was, *Yeah, sure!* She thought it a nice gesture on his part, but she certainly never for a moment believed that it was actually a sincere invitation. So she said, "Thank you very much. I'm sure you'll get news from my boss. I realize you're very busy, but I appreciate the thought."

Bill responded, "No, no, no. I would really like you to drop in when you are in Toronto."

Later, Charlotte asked some colleagues what they thought. "Should I let him know when I'm going to be in Toronto or not?" Their responses: "No, I don't think so."

A few months later, when Bill heard that Charlotte had been in Toronto, he called and said, "Now, Charlotte, I understand you were in Toronto, but I don't have anything on my calendar from Alice that shows you gave me a call."

A Holistic Perspective: Pensioners Get a Raise

When Bill dealt with an issue, he did not compartmentalize it but rather recognized its place in the whole picture. He also saw how even the seemingly smallest things related to the big issues. Moreover, Bill refused to buy into the traditional logic that a leader needs to make trade-offs between conflicting goals or different stakeholders. "There are many constituencies—customers, employees, financial shareholders, the community—but I believe you can do it all." Flexibility is essential; priorities cannot be set in stone. "One day the customer may be first, but another day, we may need to focus on something else."

How Bill and the company dealt with pensioners is just one example of this viewpoint. He saw them not merely as former employees, but as people who were also customers and potential champions for the company. Their having mixed feelings about the company was something to address.

Thus, Bill saw pensioners as stakeholders too. "They built the company. So I focused on pensioners—to help them but also the company. I wanted them to be well disposed toward the company. They hadn't been communicated with. Pension increases had been denied. They were not a happy band.

"My job was to be fair. They're part of our family. So we gave them an increase in their pension. We got a tremendous response."

In another instance, the financial people told Bill that the company should deduct $25 to $50 per person from pensioners' checks for increases in medical costs. That didn't sit right with him. He told them to go back and look at it again. "Isn't there a way we can reduce these amounts? I have a number in my head—$10 for a single person and $15 for a family.

"The point was: We weren't even in the black yet, but the employees were getting bonuses. Why can't we share that? I wanted them to look harder because it affects integrity and values."

"It permeates the organization. If you treat someone poorly, that's not the only person it affects."

So they charged pensioners the smaller amount, using a reserve to fund it.

Investing CEO Time in People

Bill held "Breakfast with Bill" meetings at headquarters once every month. Invitations went out to all employees at that location each month. Several dozen people showed up for each meeting, shared coffee, and then Bill talked about the company and answered their questions.

He went around the country at least twice a year to meet with all employees. He put together a presentation about the company—how it was doing and what initiatives were being launched. His visits included his presentation, answering questions, and informal time just meeting with people. People would ask, "Why don't you come out more often?"

Bill did not want to overdo it. "It's got to be special when you go out there, but you can't let two years go by. They knew that I was going to come out, and there would be fifty people in the room waiting for me. They would have questions. Besides the PowerPoint presentation, I'd have a couple of stories and some jokes. And I'd always have a new message. I'd have a theme that I wanted to get across—usually one that they weren't thinking about yet."

"I was trying to get the message out in a variety of ways. But it had to be a personal method. People would say, 'I would never have expected a CEO to spend this much time with us.' But what does a CEO do with his/her time? I'm fairly efficient with my time. But that was an important thing, communicating the vision, the values, the objectives, and where the company was going."

Often the "little" communications had the greatest impact. A woman who met Bill that first day at the sales conference later wrote to him when he left the company:

> *"You drove through that snowstorm three years ago to join my sales kick-off, and I vividly remember that day.... The next time I saw you was in the spring, walking along the street. You stopped and greeted me by name. We had met months ago and I was just one of over a thousand faces and names!*
>
> *I remember (how could I forget?) when you called to thank me for the work I had done on the company's behalf as you were signing off on commission cheques... I hung up on you after putting you on hold two times and all round not believing it was you but (rather) a practical joker!! Most people would call that a 'career-limiting move' but you just said it was one of the funniest things that had ever happened to you!"*

The People Side of the CEO Role

"Where you spend your time is a matter of judgment," Bill observed. "It's very subjective. Where are you going to spend your time, how much time are you going to spend there, and how efficient are you in doing it? And yet, you don't want to be one of these people who say, 'Okay, your fifteen minutes are up.' Generally speaking, people understand, and if you say you have only fifteen minutes, they will respect that and will not go over that time."

Bill believed that one of his most important roles was to create and nurture important relationships. Thus, he organized his schedule in a way that best enabled him to talk individually with employees. One executive of the company wrote Bill when he retired to express how meaningful this experience was:

> *"You have taken a personal interest in so many people's careers in this organization. It really makes a difference to know that you took such an active interest in my career. That's so much a part of why I've wanted to stay at AT&T Canada. You have really made the company feel like a place that people hate to leave."*

"There are some CEOs who are always in their office," Bill later reflected. "I wanted to be available and connected. Alice Coleman, my assistant, knew that there were certain things that were priorities. I sat with her once a month to go over these priorities. She participated in creating the plans for the year, and we would talk about her role.

"I never wanted an assistant who would be a buffer between me and whomever I had to talk to. As my assistant, Alice received a lot of calls. I spent a lot of time with her so that she would know how best to handle incoming calls and requests. She was able to rearrange my schedule when one of our account representatives called and said, 'I've got this proposal that we're making to this company.' I wanted the word out that any time a sales rep had a proposal and they thought it was necessary for me to be there, they should give me a shout.

"People use the 'I'm busy' excuse all the time. And the higher they are, the more they can get away with it. If you're the president and you're late for a meeting, people say, 'Oh, he was probably doing something else important.' Maybe he was just having a cup of coffee.

"But the higher you are," Bill continued, "the more powerful it is when you don't use the excuse." When the leader shows up on time, a powerful message about the importance of people and issues is conveyed. "I made it a point to use the office of the CEO to try to set examples. When I said the meeting would start at 9:00 o'clock, it did."

Enthusiasm and Optimism

Bill's approach was to encourage and inspire. When meeting with groups of employees, for example, he would convey the message: *Look* at what we can accomplish together, and *you're* just the people to do it!

He was able to take a lot of the things that people thought were disadvantageous and turn them into an advantage. "Sure, there are an awful lot of bad things that will happen to you, but what matters is how you look at them, and how you deal with them. You roll with them, you fend them off or, if you can, you turn them into an advantage.

"I turned skepticism and cynicism into an advantage. I used the Jujitsu metaphor. Jujitsu is all about using the force of your opponent to combat your opponent.

"That's the way I handle these seemingly disadvantageous events. And they happen everyday. The competitor will do something in the marketplace, something will happen to some part of your company, there's always a facility failure. How do you turn that into an advantage? How do you find ways to do that?

"Communicating that mentality throughout a company is key. But you also have to succeed. You need to combine evidence of some success with the message, 'I told you we were going to succeed.' And if we did it in the right way, we would succeed wildly. The more you tell people, 'It's going to happen' and it starts to happen, the more they start to believe. And it's this guy who's helping us succeed. And he's sharing the rewards."

Bill worked at getting enthusiasm down to the grassroots. While there were many ways of doing this, the process was fueled by Bill's contagious enthusiasm and positive can-do outlook. "There's no silver bullet. I was successful because I was enthusiastic myself. People could argue that I was overly enthusiastic. But if you've got a team that is down in the dumps, what kind of leader do you want for your organization? You want honesty, but you also want enthusiasm and optimism about the future. I spent a lot of time communicating that positive outlook."

A salesperson later wrote:

> *"When I first started here as a Residential CSA, you came to visit us in one of our training classes to welcome us and share your vision for this company. By the end of your address, we could hardly wait to get out there and start working. You filled us with so much enthusiasm and excitement!*

We were so pleased that you had taken the time to come and see us, to talk and to listen."

Discipline and Focus

Reflecting on the power of leadership presence, Bill observed, "Sometimes people see a CEO like me who has energy and cares about people, and they think there's nothing underneath. They think that this is just fluff. But there has to be a very strong, well designed infrastructure. What I put in place was an infrastructure of process and of people. Once you've done that, you can go further and take other steps.

"None of this is the hardest work you'll ever do. It's important work. It takes discipline. It takes focused efforts, but it's not that hard. In fact, it's fun when you see what the purpose is: making employees better and making companies better."

CHAPTER 7

SUPERCHARGING THE MANAGEMENT SYSTEM

"I'm down here rowing, and I don't know where the heck the ship's going. Tell me what this is about, don't just give me orders." Sound familiar? Most people need a structured environment in which to work. Often, however, we resent and feel stifled by structure, not because it is unnecessary, but because it is overdone. In yearning to be free of this overbearing structure, we think we want no structure.

Even though Bill was now a CEO, he remembered that when *he* was an employee, he needed both structure and freedom. He needed a basic underpinning, a rationale. Then he needed to be left alone. He knew from his earlier experience that if you give employees a good enough rationale and then let them go on their own, they might actually be able to do something better than what their managers had told them to do. He also believed that most people want a logical infrastructure for their job and for the whole company.

This meant Bill needed to create a management system that would supply this kind of infrastructure. He wanted to be able to say to all his people:

Now go do it. I'm not going to watch you. I want you to figure out a way to do your job better than anybody else ever did—a way that makes you comfortable and that maximizes everything. And I'm going to bet that the more information I give you and the more I leave you alone and the more incentives I give you to make it worth your while to do that, the better off we're all going to be.

How can leaders build that kind of empowering (and freeing) philosophy into a management system? In this chapter, we'll see how Bill built just such a management system for Unitel/AT&T Canada LDS, and how his management team used it to make needed strategic decisions (involving all senior executives), implement those decisions rapidly, get steady feedback on the company's performance, and make adjustments in strategy, programs, and processes rapidly.

In essence, Bill figured out how to create sustainable competitive advantage through the management system itself.

Toward Alignment and Interdependence

Without an effective management system, companies suffer and have an uphill battle bringing about major change and improved business performance. The Balanced Scorecard Collaborative determined in a survey they conducted that:

- 95 percent of a typical workforce **does not understand** its organization's strategy;
- 90 percent of organizations **fail to execute** their strategies successfully;
- 86 percent of executive teams spend **less than one hour per month discussing strategy;**
- 70 percent of organizations **do not link** middle management **incentives to strategy;**
- 60 percent of organizations **do not link strategy to budgeting**.

When he started out, Bill met with the managers of every unit once a month to review results, where they were going, and their projections for the future. He used these regular meetings, not only to see how managers were doing, but also to offer encouragement. In addition, he was forced into acting as a liaison among senior executives when strategic issues required that they communicate with one another.

Bill began to realize the limitations of this silo approach to governance: There was no opportunity to create greater understanding, collaboration, and commitment, nor was there a way to get the input of all the people he had brought into management. If he were to continue this approach, he would be stretched thin, and the company would not likely benefit from the total talent represented in the top management team. Consequently, the company might continue to spin its wheels and fail to turn around the dire situation.

I want people to break out of the mold they're in, but you don't break out of the mold until you start out with an infrastructure. You can't have a company with 2800 people just "doing their own thing." There is a certain basic infrastructure that is needed, and people have to buy into that structure. If they can't buy into that, then we don't have alignment.

After a year on the job, Bill created a new system for managing the company, one designed to channel the energies, abilities, and knowledge of people throughout the organization toward meeting the company's long-term strategic objectives. He included these five components in this new management system:

The Vision and Mission. These would be used not as some framed statement somewhere, but whenever they were considering major strategic decisions, and even more important, whenever new initiatives and resulting performance were being communicated throughout the company.

The Values. As we saw in an earlier chapter, creating the values became an early company-wide effort. These values would be used continually in making decisions about policies, strategies, promotions, and rewards.

Corporate goal. To provide a focus for the work of the management team, Bill defined the company's goal: "sustained profitable growth."

Business plan. The plan had to define the strategies for achieving the corporate goal, the programs for carrying out the strategies, and include a budget with revenue projections and their anticipated source, expense budgets, and capital expense budgets—all aligned with the business strategy.

Performance drivers. Bill identified five areas in which the company had to excel:

Growth: attracting and retaining customers

Operations: providing high quality service at an efficient cost

People: attracting, growing, motivating and rewarding people

Financials: the financial manifestations of all of the above

External Environment: relationship with the community, including the government

Measures. Measurements would be used to communicate objectives, targets, and performance. Bill used the Balanced Scorecard approach† as a starting point, with measures developed for each of the performance drivers. This provided a powerful way to help people to understand what each of the measures meant and how it related to the company's overall strategy and goals. He wanted the measures to be incorporated into the business plan, expense budget, capital expenditure budget, and each manager's strategy.

---

†"The Balanced Scorecard is a management system that can channel the energies, abilities, and specific knowledge held by people throughout the organization toward achieving long-term strategic goals.... The Balanced Scorecard translates an organization's mission and strategy into a comprehensive set of performance measures that provides the framework for a strategic measurement and management system."—*The Balanced Scorecard,* Kaplan & Norton, Harvard Business School Press, 1996

Those were the components, but Bill wanted a system to bring together all of the pieces at both corporate and operational levels. This would include the decision-making process involving senior managers in a joint endeavor, with each person contributing his or her perspective, questions, and, ultimately, their vote.

Conventional management practices do not integrate those components well. For example, as the CEO working within a conventional management system, you would work closely with, say, the president of the Commercial Business unit on a possible merger with another enterprise. You and she would know exactly what you want to do—buy the company—and would decide to do it. Then, you would get everybody together and say, "We are acquiring XYZ Company." Then you might add, "Oh, by the way, they have 250 people." The HR person would then say, "It would have been nice to know about this two to three months ago because… you know what we were doing regarding people?" And on and on.

By contrast, under the management system Bill was creating, everybody would have a piece of the action—even in making big strategic decisions. The people developing a strategy would let others know that a certain strategic move was coming down the pike, and they would all work on it together. At an early stage, for example, the tax lawyer might say, "Have you considered these tax implications?" Or the HR person might ask, "How is this going to impact our relations with the union?" Having a piece of the action means working as part of a team and being responsible to the whole company.

Collaborative Decision-Making

This is how Bill described what he wanted from his senior executive team:

> *Take eighty percent of your time and devote it to your function. You're empowered. You go do it. When we talk, we'll focus on results—not plans, actions, programs. That will greatly cut down on the time that I need to spend with you on operational issues, and it will free up your time too. The other twenty percent belongs to the company. You'll use it to participate in strategy development and decision-making that affects the company overall. You will act as advisors to each other.*

To provide a forum for these activities, Bill created four councils, one for each of the four primary performance drivers.

The Growth Council was charged with ensuring that strategy and operations were aligned and with figuring out how to grow the business profitably by focusing on markets and customers, new products and services, and on possible alliances. The head of Strategic Planning led this council.

The Business Process Council, led by the head of Operations, was charged with planning and leading the efforts to improve quality and efficiency and provide increased value to the customer.

The Professional Development Council was responsible for attracting, motivating, developing, and rewarding people. The head of Human Resources was in charge of this council.

The Balanced Scorecard Council was responsible for monitoring and guiding overall performance. Bill led that council.

All senior managers were members of *each* council. Each council met for three hours per month. All senior managers were expected to attend; Bill was asking them to spend a total of twelve hours a month in these meetings. People at lower management levels often were invited to participate as well, because they were involved in projects or issues on the council's agenda, and some meetings—for instance, when professional development issues were addressed—would be open to anyone interested.

As an example, in Bill's view, if you were head of External Affairs and your job was to promote the company's image and a new initiative was being considered in some part of the company, your participation was important. In Bill's words:

> You don't know the first thing about how the local telephone business works. You're not an engineer. But you don't have to be. You're an intelligent, bright person who can participate, ask questions. And also be certain that the thing you're responsible for "down here" (on the chart) is considered: If we do this, how will it affect the image of the company? How will it affect our employees? And how will you communicate this? So I want you to think about that—your own part of the company, your own responsibility. But I also want you to say, "If we do this, will we not forgo some other things?" I want you to be an intelligent member of a leadership team, asking good questions and having the person who's proposing this answer.

Council meetings varied in their purpose: some were informational, others were for input, and still others were for decision making. Everyone in the senior group had a vested interest in issues before the councils and participated actively. A new product or service, for example, would be brought to the Growth Council and looked at from Marketing, Operations, Customer Service, and HR perspectives.

Bill avoided the "paralysis of analysis" disease that afflicts many management groups by making clear which meetings were preparatory and which ones were for decision making. "This month," he would say, "you'll get a presentation. But next month, we're going to be prepared to make a decision."

He did not want people sitting on their hands so they later could say, "No, no, I wasn't involved in *that* one." Everyone was involved; no one got to sit on the fence. When individuals came to Bill and said, "I've got concerns," he would respond, "I've got concerns about *everything*. But we have to make a *decision*." Some people were good decision makers. Others would focus on their concerns. Bill understood that: "Give me your concerns, but understand that we have to act. I need a 'yes' or 'no.' It can't be a 'maybe.'"

Issues identified by one council often became the primary responsibility of another council. The Growth Council, for example, concluded that in order to attract new customers, the company needed to shorten the time needed for sign-up. In order to keep customers, the company needed to improve its billing process. Both issues fell within the domain of the Business Process Council.

The Balanced Scorecard Council identified many of the issues sent to other councils. Each month council members reviewed all of their Balanced Scorecard measures, which were colored in red, green, or yellow to convey the level of performance. Green meant results were on target and meeting plans. Because of time constraints, they did not dwell on the green items but made sure they understood them, acknowledged the work effort, and then moved on to items which required their immediate attention, i.e., those colored yellow or red.

Bill had a philosophy of management responsibility:

> *When you stand up and say something is "red," that doesn't mean you failed. That means you're telling the facts. As a matter of fact, we want you to tell us it's red, even when it's merely close to being red, because we don't want to hide these things from each other. The important thing is to be able to stand up and say, "This is red and I'm working on it. I am trying to fix it, but I need some help." We're all here to help.*

Senior managers began to feel good about being part of the process, truly involved in charting the company's future. Moreover, there was no passing the buck. If, for example, the head of the Commercial Business unit believed that poor customer service was affecting performance, the customer service person was there to discuss it.

Bill was ultimately responsible for key decisions but wanted his team to be part of the process. The councils made this possible. Sometimes a decision would be primarily one person's. If it was a network-related decision, for example, then the network head would have the greatest influence. But having a discussion and developing consensus regarding what was to happen was most important. Although not all decisions could be made by twenty-five people, Bill wanted to have everybody's input. He saw his CEO role not so much as decision maker but as creator of a decision-making *process* that would tap the best of his team.

Bill envisioned an integrated management system that looked like this:

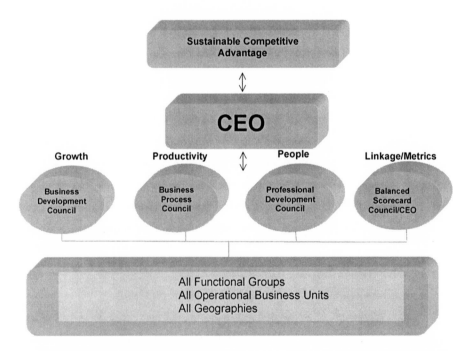

To underscore his philosophy that every senior manager was responsible to help the whole team—and company—succeed, Bill designed the bonus system so that executive bonuses were determined by how well the company as a whole performed and not by how well each senior executive's piece performed. All senior managers were paid out of the same performance bonus pool. Of course, there were disputes. People in business units that were doing very well would come to Bill and say, "We're carrying so and so," but he would not be swayed. In the new system, *everyone* had a financial incentive to help their colleagues succeed.

Energizing Practices

Some of the participants in the Unitel/AT&T Canada turnaround credited the strategic management system for the speed and depth of Unitel/AT&T's turnaround. Yet many companies have made efforts to support alignment, empowerment, and collaboration and have not achieved the kind of rapid improvement in business performance that Bill and his team were able to do. What in Bill's approach to creating and leading an integrated management system made the difference?

Energy flow. In essence, Bill facilitated the flow of energy from the sources—Mind, Body, Emotions, Heart, Will—that fuel individual performance. He did this by promoting practices that require integration of the (inner) human and (outer) material dimensions of business. Five practices in particular stand out:

> *Discipline.* The calendar for council meetings was set once a year on consultation with all participants, so everybody knew when and where each meeting would take place. Participants received agendas well in advance of meetings and were expected to be prepared. Each meeting was to be efficient and run without interruption. It would end on time. If Bill had the floor when the meeting was scheduled to end, he would stop talking and the meeting would be over. Council members were excused from meetings only if a customer needed help or if there was a family scheduling conflict.
>
> *Such practices focus the* Will *of participants. Expectations were not only clear but also met; people knew what they needed to do*
>
> *Information sharing.* The management councils engaged all concerned parties in strategic decision making. Making the right decision depended upon the open exchange of information. Bill would say, "The more you break down the blockage of information, the more you empower an organization. Everybody becomes smarter

because the information helps them understand where the company is, where it's going, what plans we have, etc. They don't understand everything, but it's a heck of a lot more than when just the CEO has meetings with all these people individually."

Information engages the Mind *when given context and meaning. Sharing information taps the* Emotions—*"I am valued"—and may also touch the* Heart—*"I can contribute to the greater good."*

Bias for action. Analytically based and action-oriented meetings drove change. Bill stressed the importance of taking action, even in the face of unresolved concerns. "I want to convince people that if they do not take prudent risks, then they will never step out. If I encourage you to take risks, you fail, and I then respond by saying, 'I told you to take a risk, I know, but you fell, and now I'm going to have to punish you for that,' they'll never do it again. I want to instill an attitude of 'If you're not taking risks—and you're not failing sometimes—then we're not succeeding.'"

To take action without fear of failure releases bounds on Will. Prudent risk taking engages the Mind in decision making, but it also taps our courage—and energy of Heart. We ask, "What are the risks? How do they weigh against need?" And we check with the Body. "Can this be done?" Having responsibility for decision making generates positive Emotions like pride and enthusiasm and opens the Heart. "I can make a difference."

Holistic approach. Bill's management system aligned and integrated the company's various units. People were no longer confined to their particular spheres but addressed issues at the organizational level as well, which allowed them to see where they fit in the company as a whole. Data on performance at the unit level and of the company overall not only permitted an appraisal of the effects of change but also demonstrated how everything was connected.

Awareness of the parts and of the whole, as well as one's place in that whole, opens the mind to new horizons. Similarly, interconnection expands the Heart's realm—"There is greater opportunity to contribute than I realized."

Collegial spirit. The management councils called for teamwork among senior managers. For success to result, people had to be honest, supportive, and respectful with one another. Bill said, "If we believe in our values—respect for individuals, integrity, and so on—that is the way we will operate in these council meetings. The way we treat each other in these meetings will be a signal to the rest of the organization of how we operate as a team. If we sit in this room and 'shoot the messenger,' then that will spread throughout the organization, and everyone else would be treated this way. I want each of us to behave as if the rest of the company were sitting right here watching."

Working with others to achieve shared goals opens the Heart. We are able to say, "I am part of a community, I am here to help." It also taps Will: "I know that I can help." Mutual support, especially when it leads to success, liberates our Emotions: "This is fun! I'm proud of what we've accomplished and want to do more." This reinforces the attractiveness of collaboration.

In brief, Bill created an integrated strategic management system that called on senior managers to help lead the company and to work collaboratively to develop and oversee the implementation of specific strategies and policies to grow the company, to improve quality, to grow people, and to tap the Human Energy Capital that ultimately increased morale, profitability, and the value of the company—all within a framework of an inspiring, far-reaching vision and high ethical values.

CHAPTER 8

QUALITY AND A CULTURE OF CONTINUOUS IMPROVEMENT

Unitel's new strategy called for turning from low prices to high quality in order to attract commercial and high-end residential business at higher prices. This radical shift in strategy would require a major transformation in the company's mindset and culture. In its desperate attempt to survive, a company that had been concentrating solely on cutting costs would need to morph into a culture that continually sought ways to create greater value for the customer.

Everybody in the company needed to focus on quality. So Bill set out to instill the quality philosophy throughout the organization. He visited all locations to talk about the role of quality in building a company that achieves sustained profitability and about the ways increases in quality would benefit individuals, as well. He also wrote articles about quality for *Strategic Moves*, Unitel's newly created company newsletter.

Bill stressed that the improvement effort would not be just about improving operations. "It's about empowerment, customer service, and morale," Bill would say. "Most of the things you want for a company you can get through quality and process improvement.

"Think about it this way. If you're in a job that only gives you a piece of the process and you don't know what the other pieces are or the ultimate reason for the process, and no one is in charge of making sure that the whole process works efficiently, then you've got to be stressed out.

"Your supervisor probably cannot make a difference. Why? Because he or she has no process for that. If I'm involved in a situation where customers wait eighteen days for activation of a service they have ordered, just one person cannot change it.

"A bunch of systems in different parts of the company contribute to the process. While individual pieces may work, the combination does not—

particularly when viewed from the customer's perspective, rather than the traditional internal perspectives like security and work flow efficiency. The only answer is to bring everybody involved in the process together to work on it, to set some realistic objectives, and then go achieve them.

"There are so many models out there on how to do it. If you're doing it one way, there's probably another company doing the same thing better. All you need to do is find out what they're doing and see if it makes sense for you."

Writing later, well into the quality effort, in *Strategic Moves*, Bill put it this way:

"Becoming a quality company is not simply a matter of improving our processes or developing superior products. Nor is it something that can be achieved by throwing resources and manpower at a specific problem within the organization.

"Quality is not a means to an end, a department within the company, or an operational discipline that we should adhere to. Quality is a way of doing business—even a value, no different from integrity, customer service, or teamwork.

"To thrive, a company's quality program must have two distinct attributes:

1. Employees must buy into the initiative and take a stake in its ownership. This, of course, requires a change in overall corporate culture and mindset of every employee; and

2. It is imperative that corporate goals to improve quality are aligned with the overall vision, mission, and strategic goals of the corporation. Matching business objectives with quality goals can be achieved only when everyone knows his or her role within the organization and takes a stake in the company's success."

Shaping the Process

The place to invest in quality was Unitel's infrastructure, but how and where?

Larry Hudson, head of Operations, and his organization led the way with quality improvement teams. Later, after Bill introduced his system for managing the company, the top management team also became involved, providing that second attribute Bill mentioned in the *Strategic Moves* column (above)—the alignment of quality improvement efforts with the company's overall mission and strategy.

The quality program eventually included the following elements:

Quality Improvement Teams. Employees formed teams to drive improvement in a process or were responsible for ensuring improvement in a quality measure. A team was typically sanctioned by a Quality Council (see below) and functioned for the time needed to achieve a quality goal or solve a problem. These teams functioned like SWAT teams. They were there to fix particular problems. They may or may not get together beyond that problem.

Process Improvement Teams. Cross-functional teams were responsible for managing and improving processes from end to end. Teams were sanctioned by a Quality Council and were responsible for determining benchmarks to measure the ongoing success of their efforts. A Process Improvement Team was typically a permanently established group. Process Improvement Teams provided the day-to-day, mid-level management of the work. Process Improvement Teams were permanent "owners" of the process. They did the analysis and benchmarking, constantly looking for ways to improve the process. They decided what needed to be improved. Then they would tell a Quality Improvement Team, "Here's the problem and the objective." So there could be several Quality Improvement Teams working for a single Process Improvement Team.

Quality Councils. A group of senior management employees provided vision and leadership for the improvement of one or more business processes or subprocesses. Each Quality Council served as the steering committee for an area or a piece of business, including for example, one for the whole customer experience and one for the "people process"—the Human Resource process.

Executive Quality Council. This council, consisting of the entire Senior Leadership Team and led by Larry Hudson (who was supported by Bill), was responsible for overall leadership and implementation of the company's quality program. Its members focused on achieving long-term growth by asking what aspects of quality need to be improved in order to attract and keep customers? This council met every month.

People outside the company often would say, "Wow. That's a lot of extra work!" But it wasn't. This way of managing was deliberately not added to an existing management system. In most companies there are Operations Review meetings. In AT&T Canada, the Quality Councils replaced that. This different management structure emphasized the quality objectives and achievement.

One advantage of this management system is that it is holistic, dealing with individual areas and issues in a way that ties them together with the rest of the company. And it provides a kind of umbrella under which new management techniques can be utilized.

Quality Improvement Teams

One of the early and important quality improvement efforts focused on the customer. Thus a Quality Improvement Team charged with addressing the customer examined the key dimensions of customer satisfaction. They studied how customers interacted with the company and identified needs for improvement. How long does it take to get an order in? What's the quality of transmission over time? How many times does the customer have difficulty? What's their interaction with customer representatives? What's their billing experience? What turns customers on? What turns them off?

They also gathered all the information they could find about customers. And they collected information on competitors and benchmarks. Then they picked the twenty major processes in the company, including two major ones—the network and customer service, plus others, for example for HR and Sales.

Quality teams were formed, and team members trained in preparation for studying their assigned process from beginning to end and finding ways to make improvements. Each quality team then brought in consultants who helped them to go through every one of the processes and map them, further enhancing the likelihood that team members would be successful in finding ways to streamline and improve processes.

Supporting the Process

Bill and his management team made a conscious decision not to provide quality improvement training to everybody all at once. Rather than provide such training and expect it to be useful anywhere in a company, Bill wanted managers and their people first to identify where they needed improvement and to define what performance they wanted. Next, team members would be selected. Only after this would they get training.

Saying, "As soon as you get on a quality team, we'll put you through the training" produced a desire for training among those who sought to join quality teams. Instead of being an end in itself, the training had a purpose. It was also more action-oriented than usual because people were learning techniques they would use immediately.

The reward system encouraged people to build quality improvement into their work. Their performance appraisal asked, "How did Joe do last year in terms of innovation and contribution to quality improvement?" This applied to evaluating leaders as well. "What quality improvement efforts were there in your operation? What were the results? How many of your people were involved?"

The Process in Action: Upgrading Customer Service

Unitel's customer service was a hodgepodge of systems and processes. Ripping out all the existing systems in order to install a new one would have been best but was impossible because the company could not suspend operations while that was being done. It would also take hundreds of millions of dollars—money the company did not have.

Bill wanted a system that could respond quickly and effectively to the need for changes, such as when a business unit wanted to introduce a new service. Normally when a new system was needed, the systems people would define the requirements in detail and then build them into a program. In some companies, this process could take as long as a year. Bill wanted to get that time down, so that new products and services could be introduced in ten weeks. And he wanted to get that kind of response without jeopardizing other projects.

The Executive Quality Council determined the priorities for improvement. That made upgrading customer service a joint decision, with Bill responsible for the goals and the Executive Quality Council responsible for doing what was needed to achieve them. As Bill saw it, "We're all together, and we know that this is a priority, and priority means we commit the resources and we follow up on it."

Bill set high expectations. He asked departments, teams, and individuals, to set high goals. Wherever he went, he talked about the quality improvement efforts already underway, challenging people to find areas that needed improvement in quality and to volunteer to join a team to work on that. He publicized teams and their efforts in talks around the company and in the company newsletter. Public celebrations of team accomplishments fueled people's pride, confidence, and momentum.

Streamlining the Order Entry System

The Customer Service Quality Council set a priority early on to fix the order entry system. They put together a Process Improvement Team for the provisioning of customers. The team was fully integrated, with members from marketing, sales, and billing.

The existing sales order process was relatively new. But the sales people were saying, "It's too complicated. We want to be able to get that order in immediately without error." It also took eighteen days to get a new customer into the system, during which time many of the customers were picked off by competitors and never even made it into the AT&T Canada system at all.

The Customer Service Project Management Team called on the company's Billing Production department to improve the order entry system. (The Order Entry department directly set up the new customer's information. They were experiencing problems in getting a "clean order" entered into the system. How the order was entered determined the customer, what account would be billed, and what services would be billed. Problems in that information caused problems later in billing.)

The Billing Production Department had already begun using an innovative approach to address important issues as a group: the Six Thinking Hats™ methodology developed by Edward de Bono. This methodology incorporates six modes of thinking (information, feelings, caution, benefits, creativity, and guidance), which helps everyone to participate, stay focused, and move into areas where they may feel uncomfortable. Pat Anderson, the company's Billing Production senior manager, observed dramatic results, including not only a fifty percent reduction in the time needed for staff meetings but also a real buzz of excitement and sense of empowerment in everyone.

After seeing the group's enthusiasm, Anderson decided to challenge the team to use Six Thinking Hats to generate ideas that would help them meet their departmental goals for cutting costs, improving productivity, and boosting customer satisfaction. "I issued the challenge and they took it from there," she said. "They came up with the ideas and formed their own work groups to tackle the issues they wanted to run with. The only criteria I set were that the ideas had to be fairly straightforward and inexpensive to implement."

Team members discovered that making even small changes to a process could result in big savings in both costs and productivity. Their efforts yielded payoffs on several fronts:

- By tracking and working on process-related defects, the team achieved a forty-percent drop in defects within a year.
- They streamlined production processes, in some cases by as much as fifty percent.
- They developed initiatives that saved the company more than $100,000 annually.

To determine how to reduce the time from accepting a new customer to getting that customer into the system, the team first looked at why the process took eighteen days. In weekly quality meetings, using Six Thinking Hats, metrics, and quality techniques, the team analyzed the existing system from beginning to end and then began making changes.

Over a two-year period they succeeded in shortening the process to three and a half days. To do this, they had to do things like get the sales people to verify the names carefully; get competing telephone companies to do their part in letting go of customers, which in part meant getting the companies to adhere to legal requirements; introduce new technology and software to get from six or seven days down to three; and institute third-party verification.

When the Process Improvement Team met to celebrate its success in reducing the time required to get a new customer into the system to three days, Bill saluted its achievement. "This is a great accomplishment."

Then he held up two fingers.

Team members said, "You want it down to *two days?*"

"No, I think we can do it in two *hours,*" Bill replied. "I know there is a cost to every improvement. But I just called one of our competitors, and they told me they could get me in their system in two hours. Why can't we do that, too? If we're going to have the kind of quality service we need to attract customers, we need to do as well as competitors."

So the team raised its bar again, eventually getting it down closer to the competitive benchmark. Further reduction was hampered because they did not have every element under their control, as they relied on regulators to make the switch on their schedule.

A Remote Call Center Wins an Award

Charlotte Daigle-Basque joined Unitel in the winter of 1995. She had worked for New Brunswick Power for twelve years, rising from management trainee to district manager, but then left to start her own home-based business. During her two years at home, she missed being with people and jumped at the opportunity when she saw the Unitel ad for manager of a Credit and Collections Call Center.

The company had decided to bring the customer service function back inside the company and planned to create a call center in Edmunston in northwestern New Brunswick, a town with a high concentration of call centers handling both English- and French-speaking customers.

Charlotte traveled to Toronto for a month of training at headquarters. Because of Unitel's dire financial situation in 1995, however, the call center plans were put on hold. Instead, Charlotte spent 1995 managing a credit and collections group in Toronto. During that year, her unit improved its productivity with big gains in morale.

With the restructuring of Unitel, the company reactivated its plan to create an Edmunston call center. In January of 1996, the month that Bill Catucci started as CEO, Charlotte headed back to New Brunswick to organize the new call center.

The Edmunston call center started with forty-five people. By early April, they took their first call. In June, a grand opening ceremony was held. Bill Catucci attended and spent time getting to know the Unitel team. Also attending were community leaders and the premier of New Brunswick. The employees were excited that their CEO took the time to attend. It was just a beginning and not a very big site, so it was an honor that he felt it important to attend. They were struck with his genuine interest and approachability. They were also excited to hear what he saw as the potential for the site for the company, and they felt that he supported them and their efforts.

In other organizations that Charlotte was familiar with, you would not have seen the CEOs travel to smaller events because their calendars were so full. The fact that Bill made the trip impressed Charlotte and her team.

Bill continued to stay connected with the people of the Edmunston call center through his regular activities at corporate headquarters, and through specific checks or periodic phone calls about how the Edmunston site and the team were doing. In conversations with Charlotte, he would know all the facts about the site's performance and the morale survey. And he'd take the time to call or to send a note or to stay connected. Sometimes, he would get on the phone with the whole group, such as when they had the best overall results of all the sites on the morale survey.

The plan called for the Edmunston call center to be a five-day operation to handle the overflow from the main call center in Toronto, a seven-day operation which employed two hundred people. Right from the start, Charlotte had other ideas for the Edmunston call center. It would start as a back-up, overflow center, to be sure, but her vision was to make it the biggest and best call center in the company. Over the next two years, she and her team worked at being the best in quality, in customer satisfaction, and in employee morale.

Charlotte could have held her vision as a "someday, wouldn't it be great if…" kind of picture. She was emboldened, however, by the impact of Bill's visit and support, because she knew that such initiative is not always what a company wants. Many companies say they want employees to "think outside the box," but it is not uncommon for management to resist the idea of lower level managers working on creating a new or bigger box. The story was different at AT&T Canada.

Charlotte set the following goal with and for her group: When customers talk to us, they are wowed. When people look at our processes, they see that they make sense and that we follow through. When people look at the quality of our customer service, they know not only that we do it well and that we do it professionally, but that we also keep improving it.

When Charlotte interviewed prospective new employees, she looked for passion and values, not just skills. She trained new hires for three to five weeks so that they not only would know the processes and policies of the company, but also would practice living and expressing the company's values through their interactions with their customers. In essence, Charlotte looked for and invited the whole person to work.

She created recognition processes to let people know how important their contributions were. These included:

- Star Recognition certificates, given to associates who excelled according to customer surveys or internal quality monitoring or exceeded objectives relating, for example, to speed in assisting customers
- The Call of Fame award, given to an associate who handled a difficult customer in a way that pleased the customer yet also honored the company's financial realities
- Official Team Motivators, who would make sure everyone knew about specific successes by, for example, tying balloons on the back of the person's chair.

Recognizing how grueling the job could be, Charlotte made the job and the work experience fun. The fun part of working for the Edmunston call center consisted of such events as:

- Recognition and Appreciation Days for special accomplishments—often with food
- Dances and Valentine Day's parties, all planned by employee teams
- Participating in the local summer festival parade with an AT&T float and banners. Associates even wrote an AT&T Canada song and performed it in the parade.

In its first year, the Edmunston call center led the company in employee morale, as it would in subsequent years. Its productivity numbers and customer satisfaction also excelled.

As a result, the center doubled its staff in the second year. In December 1997, within two years of opening, the Edmunston call center became the primary call center, operating on a seven-day schedule, while the Toronto center dropped to a five-day schedule. Edmunston surpassed its sister center in number of calls in the spring of 1998.

Along with the rest of AT&T Canada, the Edmunston call center participated in the countrywide Canada Award of Excellence quality program. When the company held its celebration of the company-wide quality improvement efforts in Toronto, the Edmunston group was not able to send anyone. But Charlotte had a surprise in store for them.

Each year the Northwestern New Brunswick Industrial Commission named a "Company of the Year." Charlotte arranged for two tables for the Annual Awards Dinner, explaining to her team that since they could not attend the Toronto celebration, she wanted more associates to attend the local celebration, which would honor the Company of the Year in Northwestern New Brunswick. They knew that the award always went to a manufacturing firm that had been around for some time. After all, their call center was just an upstart company and not even in the manufacturing sector. Nonetheless, they felt honored to be there.

During the meeting, just as an associate turned to Charlotte to ask, "Hey, why couldn't we qualify for this award?" the announcement came that this year's winner was the Edmunston AT&T call center.

Sources of Success

What fueled or enabled the company's success in dramatically improving its quality? Was it the quality management system described above, with its various councils and teams? Was it the encouragement they received from the CEO and top management team? Here is what participants cited as drivers of this success:

The Outer Dimension

Participants in the revitalization of Unitel/AT&T Canada pointed to an array of practices leading to success of the quality improvement effort:

- Some said the key was **training** people to use a common problem-solving process so they could introduce solutions in a more integrated way.

    Employees received training when they had joined a team and were ready to apply their new knowledge. They were activated and engaged by the challenge. The quality improvement teams and processes focused these energies on business processes and ways to streamline them.

- Participants also credited the **discipline** of the process: using research data, developing and carrying out project plans for improvements, tracking results, and reporting regularly.

    The Executive Quality Council reviewed results regularly, which underscored the importance of the measures. Employee surveys and customer surveys, as well as operational data, gave the teams a grasp of reality; and when results fell short of targets, the teams did more analysis and developed and implemented new ideas.

- Others said the **reward system** provided an incentive to shift to a quality improvement mentality.

  Special events celebrated success and acknowledged teams' contributions, and managers' contribution to quality improvement was assessed as part of their performance reviews.

- Others pointed to the power of **teamwork**.

  Creating team goals called for developing mutual respect and support in pursuing common goals.

- The improvement effort was powered by a **culture of continuous improvement**.

  Emphasis was placed not on what was *wrong* but rather on what quality levels were *needed* to succeed and on the CEO's statement that he wanted everyone to be continually improving him or herself. "If you're not on a process improvement team," Bill would say, "You should be asking your supervisor, 'What's wrong with me? Why am I not on a process improvement team?'"

The Inner Dimension

The quality improvement effort created a **spirit of excitement, challenge, and fun.** This spirit started from the top and cascaded through the organization. The CEO set the tone, not just the focus, of the effort in many ways, particularly by being available to people and showing up at all hours to support and cheer them on.

The effort drew on the full complement of Mind, Body, and Spirit energies. It:

- engaged the energies of the Mind through training, the use of measurement and analysis, and problem solving.
- employed the energy of the Body in organizing and carrying out complex projects and, as well, drew forth more can-do energy.

- drew forth Heart energies because people internalized what had to be done to save the company, worked closely with others, and identified with customers to serve their needs even better. People found that they were serving a purpose beyond "merely" filling their functional role in a department.

- tapped Emotional energies as people built teams and worked collaboratively and in new ways with others, celebrated success, and were motivated by rewards for performance.

- called upon Will energies as employees met the rigorous demands of measurement, design, and implementation on a continual basis. This was not an effort that would be "nice" to do or just reflect well on people individually. They had to do this; otherwise, the company had no future. Will energies created the focus and discipline to facilitate that change.

Even if just one of these energies were missing, the improvement effort would not have achieved the impressive results it did. The whole person, not just the mind and body that are typically called on in improvement efforts, was engaged.

A Thousand Flowers Bloom

Once people began to understand the thinking behind the quality program and got involved, Bill saw "a thousand flowers"—quality initiatives and teams—springing up all over the place. "You don't even have to plant seeds," he said.

Bill depicted the new mindset within the organization this way: *"You are thinking quality. You are thinking process. You're sitting out in Vancouver and you go to your supervisor and say, 'You know what we need to do, we need to get some people together and look at this thing.' And it happens. That's a flower growing up. All that the CEO has done is to create an environment where that kind of thinking is rewarded."*

CHAPTER 9

A BOND OF TRUST WITH CUSTOMERS

At the time of its restructuring, Unitel was a company with low prices, low quality, and no profit.

The marketplace was essentially saying, "Long-distance services? So what? All I care about is price." Bill and his management team asked themselves: "Do we want that customer? If so, how do we go after that customer?" Also, "Who else is going after that customer, and can we compete with them?"

The Growth & Strategy Council looked thoroughly at the business and residential markets and decided they wanted customers that seek "high quality phone service with high customer service at a FAIR price (but not the lowest price)." They wanted to be able to charge more because customers would be getting more.

To succeed, they needed to answer the questions: Could the company convince the marketplace that this is the right model? What actually constitutes value and what are customers, or at least some of them, willing to pay for that value?

Value included:

- network quality and the technology driving it, plus
- the quality of customer service—a product of both technology and people.

But customer value would include an additional ingredient, something deeper that could set them apart from the competition and thereby support higher prices: the quality of the *relationship* that the company created with customers. The bottom line measure (and thus company goal) of this relationship would be trust.

Building and Measuring Customer Value

If the company was going to sell and deliver value, it would first have to define and measure it.

In fact, the Growth Council decided to concentrate on listening and trying to understand customer needs rather than sell them a product. They used a concept called Customer Value Added (CVA), which is customers' perception of AT&T Canada LDS versus the competition, measured by two major attributes: quality and price.

To create Customer Value Added, they would have to deliver value through each phase of their value chain:

- How they sell
- How they install
- How they deliver quality in the phone call itself
- How they bill

To measure the value created in each phase, they hired an outside firm to conduct regular customer surveys. The surveys asked questions about price, quality of the phone service, customer service, availability of products, and the like. They also asked, "How important is AT&T's brand?" and "What does the AT&T Canada brand mean?"

To get at the value of the relationship between the commercial customer and the company, including that underlying value of trust, they also asked such questions as:

- How do you feel about your relationship with the salesperson?
- Does your salesperson understand and listen to you?
- How well do you trust your Unitel salesperson?
- How well do you trust your service manager?
- How well do you trust your business with us?

The fact that a customer says they like the company is interesting feedback but not good enough. Council members needed to know why. Detailed questions helped answer that, questions like:

- How did you learn about us?
- When you make a long-distance call, is the line "clear"—no noise on it?
- Are you proud to be a customer of AT&T Canada because of their standing in the community?
- Is your bill accurate?
- If it's not accurate, is the matter resolved quickly and in a pleasant manner.

The evaluative criteria were created essentially by clients, via an outside market research firm which asked clients what was important. Then measurements were created, tracked, and improved for all aspects of network performance and customer service.

There were four areas on the consumer side: 1) Marketing or customer acquisition, 2) Provisioning (putting them on the network), 3) Billing, and 4) Customer service, which can take place in any one of the four areas.

The Leadership Team also needed to know how the customer saw the company relative to its competitors, and thus the surveys measured each dimension, like price or quality. A score of 1.00 meant that the company was equal to the competition, less than 1.00 meant it was worse, and more than 1.00 meant it was perceived as better. For example, a score of .90 on price and 1.10 on quality said that the company was providing a very high quality service compared to competitors but at a price that was not competitive.

The question then became: Is price or quality more important to this customer? Should we take the quality down to 1.0 and take the price down too? The answer would depend on where they wanted to be in the marketplace and its past experience.

Every month that the Growth Council met, the CVA numbers received considerable air time—far more than the financials, which were "merely" the result of all these other measures of the business.

Selling a Company, Not Just Its Technology and Product

While the company worked to improve its network technology and customer service processes, Bill began contacting existing and potential business customers.

He figured he did not have the luxury of waiting until quality had been improved. He would have to take some risks. During his first nine months, the company was still called Unitel, and he had to begin rebuilding the company's image. Competitors were saying, "Why would anyone want to do business with Unitel? They're going out of business."

Ontario was the source of sixty-five percent of the company's business. That meant that Bill could likely walk from the Toronto headquarters to thirty percent of the company's big customers, and could drive outside Toronto to fifty percent of the customers. And so he did.

He called the CEOs of the large customers and requested meetings. He wanted to go directly to customers to convince them that he was doing certain things to make sure that the company would be there for them. Bill led this effort together with George Harvey, the head of Commercial Business. Bill and George often brought individual salespeople with them to meet with customers.

He started with his own story: "I came here to turn this company around, and I've got a great management team to lead that effort. We're going to do some wonderful things. We're already working on quality. We'll be bringing you new AT&T products and services. We're going to change the company's name to AT&T Canada to reflect the upgrading of Unitel's quality.

"I'm not asking you to do anything right now. I just want to get to know you and understand your business, and let you know what my priorities are. If I don't deliver the goods, then fine, I understand why you'd want to go someplace. But if I do, I'm going to make you so successful, you will hardly believe it."

He presented the company's vision, mission, and values. Then he described the continuous improvement teams that were already at work upgrading the company's quality.

In talking about quality, Bill emphasized first the quality of the executive team and the employees of the new Unitel. Often, he brought members of the executive team with him. When he brought customers into Unitel headquarters for presentations, he called Unitel people (such as members of the customer service team) to come into the meeting. In this way, he communicated that senior people were available to customers if they needed them.

Bill's and George's concluding message to customers was, "Come on over." Or, "Stay with us. *Trust us.* You're going to see what we can do."

These meetings were powerful. CEOs of major companies were getting firsthand experience with the new Unitel management team and the new spirit of Unitel. The relationships being formed would provide an important foundation for later sales meetings to sign up existing customers to long-term contracts and to win new customers from competitors.

Over time, George and his team developed certain products and services that were better than the competitors', while at the same time Larry Hudson was making great strides in upgrading the nationwide network. They could now promise customers the highest quality services, excellent customer service, and a good—but not the lowest—price.

The Company's Story

Telecom companies place a very high value on their nationwide networks. Each wanted its network to be the best and most efficient—and be able to put its engineers in the sales presentation to say, "We've put thousands of kilometers of fiber in." That was supposed to wow the customer.

When Bill and his team started their sales meetings, companies were surprised: "You're the first company that did not start out with the network." Bill wanted to do something a little different. "Potential customers are coming in to learn about us. We have three hours. I want to use most of that to describe the company." He would display and talk about the company's vision, mission, values, and governance structure. He would tell the AT&T Canada story. He would not show a network map. Everybody had one of those.

He put the other telecom companies on the defensive by saying, "Let me tell you about our *company* and the kind of *people* we are. We want you to know about us as the *people* you're going to deal with. Remember: we're talking about a three- or five-year contract, so I want you to know who we are and what kind of company we are."

Bill also started to sell the value proposition of trust. *Trust us with your business. Why? Because this is the kind of company we are. These are the values we have. And we hire the people who exude that when they are out there.*

Finally, after Bill and his team told the company's story, they would talk about technology—for fifteen or twenty minutes.

Bill's approach worked for two major reasons: First, the story was told from the top. Hearing directly from the company's CEO made a big impression on major customers. This gave Bill and his team an advantage over competitors. Second, Unitel salespeople would be in the room, hearing the story from their CEO firsthand and seeing customers' reactions. They then would begin telling the story of the new company, including the value it was creating for customers.

CEO as Salesperson

The salespeople often said, "I need to have Bill there because the company I'm talking with wants the CEO there." They knew Bill had a sales background and that he enjoyed selling and loved to tell the story.

A lot of potential customers had "beauty contests." They would select three or four telecom companies and visit each one. They wanted to know who the companies' executives were and what they did.

It was easy for Bill to stand up in front of a team of people and tell the story, so he played to his own strengths. He talked with potential customers about the innovation process and about the company's values. He would even show them the employee surveys. Customers often said, "I wish we had a survey like that." Or, "We feel the same way that you do." Or they would ask, "How do you do your customer-value survey?"

A decision of this magnitude for a customer would often get to the company's CEO and maybe even its board. At the least, they could say about Unitel/AT&T Canada, "I met the CEO. He's committed to this. And if I want to pick up the phone and call this guy, I've got his card and his number."

Every Employee as Company Representative

Bill would also tell prospective customers, "Everybody hypes their story and feels good about their own company, just like your own children. But I invite you to go around and talk to anyone in our company. Ask them questions. Ask them about our strategy."

Typically, visiting companies would want to see Unitel/AT&T Canada's Customer Service department. They would go in and see what kind of people worked for Unitel/AT&T Canada. Bill would start off their visits by saying, "I want to do business with a company whose people believe in the company and are enthusiastic about the company. I would imagine that you do too. Now you go and talk to my people and see if they feel that way."

Because of the great enthusiasm down in the ranks, amazed customers would report back to Bill that they had talked to a clerk, and the clerk said, "I love this company!"

Energizing & Supporting the Sales Force

George Harvey made sure that every account manager had account plans for his or her customers. Periodically, Bill and George would meet with individual account managers and go over issues.

"Here's the revenue today," they might say. "Here's what we want to get. Here's the product. Here are the guys we're going after. Here's the organization. Who are the key people? Show me where I am needed. Does that mean I need to go to breakfast with that guy to get to know him a little better? What's the problem in getting them to use more of our services? How much business do they have with the other guy?"

Then they would look at the customer's organization chart and say, "That's the key decision maker. What's he like? Is he a golfer? Does he like the opera? If you invited him and his wife to the theatre, what would happen? Where do they live?"

Often, the sales representative would want to make a sales presentation to the top executive, the CEO. But it is difficult to reach the CEO. Unitel sales reps soon learned that their own CEO—as well as George, president of their Commercial Business unit—were ready and eager to help them reach CEOs and participate in the sales meetings. The message was out: "We've got a guy who's comfortable meeting customers, wants to meet customers, wants to tell our story."

One salesperson called and told Bill, "We can't get near the president/ CEO of FedEx. If you call the CEO, maybe we can get together."

Bill's response was "What's so hard about that?" He called this person, arranged a meeting, and drove out to the FedEx office with his salesperson. The FedEx people were impressed with the Unitel salesperson because he was able to get to his CEO.

Prior to the meeting, the sales rep and Bill had done their research. They said to the FedEx Canada CEO, "All your services in the U.S. are with AT&T, aren't they?"

"Yes," the FedEx CEO answered.

"Well, why don't you have AT&T Canada here?"

"The quality of Unitel stinks. You have problems."

Bill said, "Give us a shot. Let us take a look at your services. Let us make a proposal to you. You don't have to buy or do anything. You just have to listen. See if there's something that we can do because I promise you that we can do this."

Six months later, Bill returned with Larry Hudson, the chief operating officer, who described what he was doing to improve the network and how they were going to provide quality. FedEx moved their long-distance business from Bell to Unitel.

Acting in the Best Interests of the Customer

Part of Bill's strategy in attracting and retaining customers was to prove to them that the customer's success was as important to AT&T Canada as it was to them. Bill knew that for this strategy to work, they would have to mean it. It had to permeate the organization. Every once in a while, Bill would make a point of taking action that would hurt the company—and also help it.

He would tell major customers, "We're selling you high-quality customer service. Yes, we cost a little more, but we're worth it. I'm going to stand on the relationship and the fact that I want you over the long term. In fact, every once in a while, the market falls out of the bottom and when it does, if we can translate that into lower prices for you, we'll come back to you and do it. You don't have to worry. If somebody is out there providing that service at a lower price, you know what? You'll get that lower price from us without even having to ask." AT&T Canada billed that as an issue of integrity.

Bill also went above and beyond the norm in assisting customers *himself*. For instance, while on vacation in Mexico with his family, Bill learned that J.C. Chartrand of Equifax had called to say his phone service was down. Bill immediately left Mexico to meet with him, even though he had no knowledge yet of what went wrong or what was needed to fix it and prevent such failures in the future. He had only his own belief in the future of Unitel and the people. Chartrand was so impressed with Bill's response that Equifax stayed with Unitel.

As a result of efforts like these, Unitel/AT&T Canada attracted and retained such large commercial customers as IBM, AMAX, FedEx, and Equifax, plus the big banks.

Rebuilding the Residential Market

Rethinking and remaking the company's residential market began even while Bill and the Commercial Business team were focused on the commercial sector. Despite the fact that each residential customer contributed far less to sales volume than a typical commercial customer and that residential customers did not generally value or want to pay for the features designed for commercial customers, the Residential Business team created and implemented strategies to rebuild market share, attract and keep customers, and to make money doing it. They too would find ways to build powerful relationships and loyalty with residential customers.

Carole Salomon headed the Residential Business unit, which

represented about twenty percent of the company's business. When she joined Unitel in early 1996, the unit was decimated:

- Very little money was being spent on marketing, and the best people had left.
- Sales of residential service had been contracted out to a telemarketing company. There was no market research, no targeting, no advertising, and no promotion. Morale was terribly low.
- Customers were coming in based on poor selling techniques. Turnover was eight percent per month.
- During the eighteen days needed to get a new customer into the system, fifty percent of the new customers were won back by competitors.
- There was a good customer service team, but it took four or five calls to resolve a problem.
- In each process, nobody spoke to anyone else, even though it was supposed to be seamless.

While the quality teams worked on fixing many of the operational issues, the Residential Growth Council set out to rebuild the business.

Customer Acquisition

In the telecom industry, the modus operandi had been to grow customers and worry about profits later. How could Unitel grow customers *and* margins at the same time? The Residential Growth Council identified market niches to go after; in particular, ethnic groups such as the Portuguese and Chinese communities. The strategy was to become *part* of the community. They recruited salespeople from the community and involved them as part of AT&T Canada.

Price pressure in the residential long-distance market was intense. There was virtually no way to hold onto the high-value residential customer because new market entrants could easily come in and take your business away. So the council decided to seek a way other than price to compete.

Attracting better quality customers—ones that would stay longer— became their goal. To do this, the council:

- negotiated compensation with their telemarketing firm for sales people to be compensated based on verified sales and process improvement, plus a residual, determined by how long each customer stayed;
- contracted with twelve telemarketing agencies, which expanded their

sales force ten times, from 150 to 1500 people;

- treated the telemarketing firms as if they were part of the company, guiding them in hiring people with the same values Unitel had—especially integrity, teamwork, and respect. In monthly meetings with all the firms, the company's marketing people shared results, provided training, and even provided measurements. Eventually the telemarketing firm's values matched Unitel's.

Customer Retention

When phone service was a monopoly in Canada, customers were practically ignored. Once there was competition, everyone tried to acquire customers, but less effort was employed in retaining them. The Growth Council decided that they should concentrate their strategy on retention. So, Carole and her team focused on how best to hold onto customers.

Because some thirty to forty calls were needed to acquire a new customer, keeping a customer was cheaper than finding a new one. This meant providing quality service.

Unitel's prices were higher than competitors', but after a couple of years of working on quality, customers perceived its customer service as better than competitors' as well, which was a big plus.

However, the company was still not gaining on its competition.

The Customer Value Added survey looked at customers by segment. The surveys showed customers segmented by average monthly expenditure: $10 and under, $25 and under, $50 and under, etc. The analysis showed that customers using $35 or less worth of long-distance services were not profitable. If they made $100 of calls per month, they were "golden," and so the business team began to think of them as "Gold Customers."

The team decided to "invest" in those customers who were high volume callers (over $100 per month) and were not changing telephone companies frequently, figuring, "These customers will stay with us. They are ours to lose."

They decided to do an experiment. They conducted a Customer Value Added survey in which they always gave targeted customers a live person when they called in. When they looked at the results on "value for what paid" they found that they were above the competition. Their score was 1.15.

The business team then developed a special program for those customers who said, "Service is my most important factor" in the surveys. They introduced a Gold Customer level of service for these niche residential customers. Whenever a Gold Customer made $100 of calls in a month, she received a discount, like a frequent flyer award. That customer would also get a live person when she called in. And it would be a person who could deal with her problem in one phone call, without transferring her to someone else.

The business team recognized that even if the company provided superior service to price sensitive customers, these customers would still jump from one provider to another.

The team arranged that whenever a customer who valued mostly price called, that customer would go through the automated system. In effect, they gave up the high-churn customers (those customers who leave the company to go with a competitor) to the market, figuring that there was no way they could spend enough to keep these people anyway.

On the other hand, the team invited top residential customers to golf tournaments or gave them movie tickets to communicate, "We appreciate your business."

As momentum began building, the response went well beyond their expectations. With the Gold Customer program, the churn rate dropped like a stone for the segment of customers who valued service. At the beginning of the turnaround, the churn rate had been nearly fifteen percent per month. By the end of the turnaround, they had gotten that rate down to two percent.

Carole had inherited an organization that added one hundred new customers per day (though half of these never made it into the system), and this number had been trending downward. Within six months of taking the actions described above, the business unit was adding several thousand new customers per day. Why? It listened to customers, measured customer sentiment regularly and compared itself against the competition, and made strategic decisions based on the data, including selecting profitable niches and upgrading the sales force and the service.

Reflections on Success in the Market Place

Within the major markets, Unitel/AT&T Canada gained considerable ground on the competition because the company was providing good service and because there was a feeling of trust. Increasingly strong sales relationships with customers fueled much of this trust.

The relationship at the sales level was quantifiably better than the competition's, and that gave AT&T Canada the edge. Customers would say, "Your prices aren't the cheapest, and maybe we've had some issues with you in the past, but you're here every day and you listen to us."

What led to this remarkable transformation?

Reflecting on what they did to win over big customers and what his own role was in that, Bill mused, "*I thought it was a tremendous opportunity to go one-on-one with top-level people. I had to have people backing me up, but we got salespeople so enthused, so motivated, because of the financial incentives—and the ability to win. If you're a salesman, there are two things you want. You want money and you want recognition. So we were giving them money, and we were succeeding.*"

But there was much more.

Outer Drivers of Success consisted of:

- Growth Council's decisions about marketing strategy (as described above),
- Commercial & Residential Business units' surveys and measures of their customers and market niches,
- Disciplined pricing and value decisions,
- Sales force's more assertive approach emphasizing value,
- A sales incentive plan so that good sales people would stay and be financially motivated, and
- CEO involvement in strategizing about and meeting with individual customers.

Inner Driver of Success consisted of Bill's conscious effort to restore a sense of pride, excitement, and confidence within the sales ranks by:

- Attending the annual sales conference,
- Helping individual sales managers and sales representatives,
- Signing bonus checks and calling salespeople to thank them for their contributions, and
- Dropping in on salespeople to "have coffee."

This effort called forth the full range of human energies:

- *Mind*—to design and analyze customer surveys, to develop new strategies for attracting and retaining customers, and for segmenting the market
- *Body*—to put effort into all of the above
- *Heart*—to find ways to connect with customers that conveyed the company's values and built trust
- *Emotions*—to take pride in the company and in their own accomplishments
- *Will*—to stay focused and disciplined in achieving major success in customer service and sales.

Not surprisingly then, the Employee Survey showed large leaps in morale in the sales organization each year. Importantly, morale rose before the increases in revenue. In the next chapter, we will look at why this happened.

CHAPTER 10

IT'S ALL ABOUT PEOPLE

In early 1996, Unitel employees were demoralized, not only by financial losses and cutbacks, but also by the lack of strategic direction or understanding where the company was going. The Hay Group surveys of employee morale showed that the company was at the low end of five hundred North American companies.

Union people had taken pay cuts and were affected by outsourcing of jobs and cutbacks. Their anger and mistrust undermined the company's ability to provide high-quality service. When that happened, good salespeople began leaving.

None of what we saw the company achieving in prior chapters could happen without attention to the people dimension of the company.

HR as People-Builders

When Bill arrived, he immediately began talking with the few executives who were still at Unitel. He met with Judy McLeod, who ran Unitel's call centers, and asked for her views about her job, the company, and what she thought was needed for it to succeed. She briefed him as best she could, sharing her disappointment about all the good people leaving and the change in the company's culture. She said she wanted Unitel to create a culture that would attract and keep good people.

Bill then asked her what she wanted for her own future in the company. "Quite frankly, I feel burned out and discouraged," she responded. Despite her intentions not to share her frustrations, she let slip her recent experience in unsuccessfully requesting recognition through a raise in her pay. "It's time for me to make a change anyway," she concluded.

Two days later, Bill showed up in Judy's office with the senior HR person. As they handed her a five-figure check, Bill said, "This is to retroactively recognize your contributions." Since then, Judy has received much larger checks, but this one experience blew her away. "It's the whole philosophy of exceeding what people expect," she explained.

Bill met with Judy again and surprised her again, this time by asking if

114

she might like to move into the HR function. Her first response was negative. She viewed human resource personnel as functionaries who pushed paper around and put up roadblocks. "HR needs to understand the business and be part of the team—or else move on," she said.

"That's just why we need you there," Bill replied. He told her that he believed she was the right person to drive the human resource side of the business. He saw that she had a keen understanding of the organization and what it needed, as well as a unique combination of people skills and strong analytical and decision-making skills.

As Judy reflected on Bill's offer, she realized this could be a good opportunity to broaden her experience and skills. She would be functioning at a corporate level on planning issues and would have board exposure. But that was just the rational, career-oriented response. Her heart said: *This is an important opportunity to move the yardstick in terms of bringing about the right kind of culture for Unitel. I want to bring back the excitement and fun that was Unitel in the earlier days.*

So Judy became the new human resources director (and eventually was promoted to senior VP of HR). Later she would reflect, "I didn't really look at the downside. I didn't think about how difficult the job would be in the face of stiff competition for talent in the industry." They would, in fact, have lots of competition, much of it coming from the growing presence of Internet providers. Another part of telecom that was starting to take off was local exchange companies offering local service, which Unitel did not have the capability or mandate to offer at that time. Some of those companies were also trying to entice people away. Plus, all publicly traded companies could offer employees stock options which Unitel, as a private company, could not.

Perhaps most compelling, Judy saw Bill as a fellow believer in the human dimension. The previous CEO, a turnaround specialist, focused on taking *out* as many people as possible. It was clear that Bill's approach was different: he wanted to *build* people and *invest* in them.

"So," as Judy described it, "I took on the hardest job in the place. Good thing I was new at it and didn't know any better. Bill really wanted to be the HR director, so I let him help me."

The Unitel Human Resource department would now become a *builder* of the human resource, not just a custodian or rule-maker and enforcer.

Morale

Morale is a powerful force. When it is low, a company may be unable to achieve its potential; when it is high, a company may surpass its highest goals. Building morale is a strategy in itself for creating sustainable business success.

Bill saw that morale was the fuel needed to energize people to perform great deeds. He started out by listening to what people said through surveys and in his meetings with them, and then took steps to address those drivers of morale.

Some of the action would be straightforward, traditional HR fare: compensation levels, appraisal systems, incentive systems. But some of the needed action would be what *management* itself would do to *manage* better. Bill's underlying assumption was that people wanted to be led by good leaders. Providing that kind of leadership requires good communication, modeling the company's values, and other enlightened management techniques.

The starting point for working on morale was the Hay Group employee survey. The survey provided not only overall statistics for each question asked by group and location, but also individual comments, which virtually were all negative. Bill and his team reviewed the surveys and all the individual comments, asking themselves, "What do they tell us? What should we start doing? What do we do well? What should we continue to do?"

Early on, Bill told his senior leadership team, "We're going to be paid on how well we improve employee morale—and their perception of the company—in actionable, measurable ways. We will measure ourselves on how well we communicate the employee survey to our own team, how well we implement plans to improve morale, and then on the employee survey results."

The surveys, not surprisingly, showed that people gave a low rating to management's sense of direction. So Bill and his team focused early on creating and communicating an inspiring mission and a vision for the company and placed special emphasis on quality improvement and relations with customers.

The Value of Respect

Improving an organization's morale is partly about doing surveys and creating corporate-wide policies and programs. It's also about the individual actions that leaders take in their everyday interactions with people in and outside of the organization. Bill particularly wanted to communicate that employees were important, competent, and respected.

One story that helped improve the morale of a demoralized sales force came about without forethought.

During a visit to one of the outlying sales offices, Bill accompanied two sales representatives on a visit to a potential customer. The meeting went well. The company's president seemed impressed with the case for converting to AT&T Canada. Afterward, Bill returned to the local sales office while the sales reps stayed behind to discuss details of the proposed business relationship with the purchasing agent.

Once Bill was gone, the sales reps ran into a buzz saw. The purchasing agent pressed for big price concessions. When the sales reps balked, they were subjected to a barrage of abusive language and insults aimed at their company and their management.

Frustrated and near tears, one of the reps called Bill back at the sales office to ask his advice on how to handle this difficult customer. Bill's response to her was immediate and resolute: "Pack up your things and leave. We will not do business with a company that treats its vendors like this."

Then Bill called the company president and told him he was shocked and dismayed at how the AT&T salespeople had been treated. "We treat our customers with respect, and in turn we expect our customers to treat our people with respect. We are withdrawing our proposal."

This story raced through the sales organization like wildfire: their CEO had stood up for the salespeople, even at the expense of losing a major new customer. This not only stoked people's commitment to their company but also raised their self-esteem. Imagine company management putting company values above customers!

As Renato Discenza, head of Operations, later observed, "These stories become company folklore. We walked away from a potential customer who mistreated our salespeople. Who knows what the details of the story actually were? What matters is that it captures a truth about the company and its leader, so people believe it. That's what makes the story powerful. These kinds of stories tell you that this is a different kind of company"—one that values and honors its people.

In this case, the company lost the customer but built pride and determination that enabled them to make other sales. Interestingly, the company in this story shortly thereafter filed for bankruptcy!

The Professional Development Roundtable

When Bill described his plan for the governance system, Judy saw the value of having a roundtable such as the one he envisioned. Early in 1996, Judy and Bill set up a Professional Development Roundtable (PDR) to provide a forum in which she could explain HR issues and get buy-in for HR strategies and programs. All the senior executives participated in this monthly roundtable discussion. Any and every issue that related to people came to the PDR.

The Professional Development Roundtable set priorities regarding people, set goals, created action plans, and reviewed progress. Together, they identified what human resource issues they needed to address so as to help the company achieve its vision of becoming the leading telecommunications company in Canada. Then they set a long range schedule of what HR issues to address when, as follows:

Year One: 1996

In its first year, the PDR focused on what its members considered to be the highest leverage issues regarding people: communications, union relationships, the management system, and the compensation system.

> *Communications.* In the PDR's first meeting, Judy presented the Hay Group employee satisfaction survey as the starting point for planning the priorities for the Human Resource function. The survey, conducted just before Bill's arrival, showed Unitel's employee morale as one of the worst of the five hundred North American companies in the survey. The other executives had not seen it before; now they had a handle on where employee satisfaction was the lowest.
>
> Bill had his own communication vehicles: He would write letters to employees and would write a major piece for the company newsletter each quarter. He also met regularly with groups of employees. Other executives in the company were responsible for communicating about the survey throughout their organizations. Moreover, how well they did at communicating and leading was measured through employee surveys.
>
> The communications strategy for HR was to use the employee survey as a primary ingredient in introducing and reporting on HR

initiatives. Whatever policies or decisions were communicated to the organization were linked back to the survey, so that employees could see that management was focusing attention on the areas where employees were most concerned. Judy also traveled to meet with groups of leaders to tell them what HR was doing and to describe the role of managers in advancing the HR initiatives.

This emphasis on communications began in Year One and continued throughout the turnaround.

Union Relationships. Roughly a third of the Unitel workforce were union members. When Bill came on the scene, relationships with the union were horrible. The company had laid off about one thousand people and squeezed costs at the same time.

During the cutback campaign, the union took a five percent pay cut. In order for the union to agree to a pay cut, it had to get something in return, which was more members. So as part of the deal with the union, several hundred middle management engineers were moved into the union ranks. Previously, these engineers were accustomed to getting bonuses and different treatment. Now that they were in the union, they were very upset.

Despite the addition of new union members, the downsizing had particularly affected the union organization. The union downsized by seniority. The lower the seniority, the more likely one would be let go. Thus, Unitel had a very senior workforce, with average service of twenty-five years. There were very few newer union workers, and members throughout the company were disgruntled, with people either leaving the company or staying and complaining. The union members had filed nearly three thousand grievances.

Since the company had just signed an agreement with the union, management could have forgotten them for the next three years. Having concluded that improved morale was key to the company's turnaround, however, Bill and Judy identified improving union relations as a key objective for improving morale in that group of Unitel employees.

When Bill first met with members of the union, anger,

resentment, and mistrust were written all over their faces. He could not even entice them to share coffee with him. However, he got them talking about what most concerned them. They were most recently angered about the decision to outsource work to another company, which was made before Bill arrived. Such a move jeopardized union jobs.

Bill responded, "One thing I know is how to break a contract. In every contract, there's an escape clause. It usually just costs money. I'll make a deal with you: I'll break that contract, if you'll work with me and demonstrate that you can produce better results than the outsourcer company ." And so they did.

Judy took on a primary responsibility for working closely with the union. It would take years to undo the mistrust and resentment that had built up. Her secret for doing that over the three years and beyond? Working hard at building a relationship of trust. Also, recognizing that while management and the union have common interests, they have different jobs, so there will naturally be an adversarial dimension to the relationship.

To build trust, she was open about the company's situation and about the moves being considered, and she was receptive to the union's perspective. She also worked at always going into bargaining with the union with a desire for the union to win too. She felt strongly that it would not work for management to win and for the union to lose.

Performance management system. The PDR group also developed and implemented a new performance management system. Bill introduced the Balanced Scorecard method, which meant that the company's values could be incorporated into performance appraisals. Bill told his executive team, "We're not going to pay you just for results. If you achieve them in a way that actually enhances value, we'll pay you more!"

How was as important as the specific accomplishments because *how* was about the company's values. The *how* was the foundation for future accomplishments.

Job performance—the "what"—was only half of the performance equation. Why? As Judy described it, "Because you can have someone who meets all of their job objectives, but they do it either on the 'backs of people,' or without integrity. If achieving an objective is all you're measuring without looking at *how* the individual gets there, then that wasn't going to get us the company we envisioned. So we decided after a lot of discussions that measuring *how* people exhibited our values would be important."

Having a values statement with words on a page was just the start. They decided to take the approach of measuring people on how they exhibit the company's values as well as whether they meet their job objectives.

The strategy would be to reward those who were role models, deal with the people who were not, and work to move everybody in the middle to a higher standard. This required specifying how to measure the extent to which people were living the company's values.

As Judy observed, "For instance, one of their values was integrity. Another value was respect for others. So in evaluating how someone actually did—say, a sales leader—they would want to know: Did she meet her sales revenue objective? Yes. But if she did it by running roughshod over the Operations group or did it at the expense of other customers, then that individual would perhaps get full marks for their (job) performance, but would get lesser marks for the way they did it."

Team members wrestled with this. *How do you measure values?* Managers were upset initially because it sounded so subjective. *Sure, you can measure and easily tell who are the role models and the problem people. It's harder to measure and determine who's in the middle.*

To do this, they had to help managers learn how to evaluate someone on values. Some managers got it, but others didn't. The high-tech engineering people often had trouble with the seeming subjectivity of the approach. So Judy and her team worked with them—in some cases over several years—before they fully bought into this approach, not unusual considering this was a radically different performance management system than they were used to.

Compensation system. One of the clear messages of the employee survey was people's unhappiness with their compensation. Unitel's score came out well below the average of the five hundred North American companies.

Unitel had historically used a hierarchical job grading structure with thirteen different job classifications, each with its own relatively narrow band of possible compensation levels. People spent considerable time worrying about what level they were in, because the bands limited pay raises to high performers unless they moved into a different job with a higher band.

Judy's predecessors had created a new, simpler system with fewer categories with broader bands of possible compensation, which would provide more flexibility in awarding higher pay to high performers within their current band. They had not implemented it, however. Since they could not afford to give raises, they had shelved the system for better days. The only way to get a raise was to get one's job recategorized. This was a recipe for disaster, as the more nimble found ways to get their jobs recategorized, and others went years without any increase in compensation.

So early on, Judy and her new director of compensation, Norm Williams, reduced the number of grades to four—and created, implemented, and oversaw a new compensation system that would support the company's business strategy and get people focused on that, rather than on their pay grade. Though the company could not yet afford to pay above-average compensation, they created a system that was not only fair internally but also understood by everyone.

The Little Things. Although the PDR and Bill focused on the big things that would make the crucial difference in energizing the company, they also realized the power of infusing the little things with the same kind of spirit.

Bill was Judy's best idea factory regarding the human resource and how to energize it. Early on, he dropped in on Judy and said, "I've got an idea that I want you to work on. We need a company pin! I want people to feel very differently about this company." He wanted people to be proud of being part of the organization. "That's my objective. The Pin of Pride is just one way we can signal that pride."

In a day and age when most companies had let this kind of thing go by the wayside, AT&T Canada introduced the employee pin recognizing five years of service with great success.

It was a small maple leaf with the company logo in the middle made of 10-karat gold.

Once Judy had created the pin, Bill took great joy in awarding them. The company had many long-time employees. They loved receiving their pins. The pin became the company's way of sending a signal that they valued their employees and their experience with the company. This became one small way to help resurrect the feeling of pride in their company that had been squashed by years of declining company fortunes and resulting derogatory comments in the press about the company and, by inference, its employees.

Frank, an engineer, was one of many employees whom Bill got to know personally. Frank was one of those people who brightened at a "Hello," because he was definitely not someone who would expect a CEO to notice him. "That's the kind of guy Frank was," says Bill. "He wasn't looking for the limelight. But when you gave him a little attention, he just blossomed. He was in his fifties—a terrific engineer."

Frank had cancer of the stomach. Bill wanted to show respect for Frank by visiting him in the hospital. He didn't know what to expect; the cancer was progressing very quickly. When he arrived at the hospital, Frank was in bad shape, asleep. Bill said, "Please don't wake him up." But Frank's wife wanted to wake him up so that he would see Bill. Frank opened his eyes and said, "Bill," then smiled and said, "You look sharp." Bill never forgot those last words.

Bill went out to the suburbs for Frank's funeral. The place was packed. There was a huge contingent of AT&T Canada LDS people. Everyone got up and walked up to the casket. Frank's body was dressed nicely in his suit—wearing his AT&T pin. In the eulogy, the speaker mentioned how proud Frank was to be an engineer at AT&T Canada.

Year Two: 1997

Year Two continued activities of the first year and added several new areas of attention.

> *Recognition program.* In Year Two the HR department took the service pin to pensioners.
>
> Unitel had a huge number of retirees—all part of the legacy of the company, plus the changing technology that took over the roles of people. There were many early retirements. For its size, the company had a large number of pensioners—on the order of 500 people with fewer than 3000 employees.
>
> The pensioners felt disenfranchised. Many had been forced out early. Many felt that they had been tossed out without much ceremony. They weren't feeling valued. They were also worried about their pensions. Many came and talked with Bill, Judy, and others.
>
> Often companies get into conflict with pensioners, viewing them as just one more constituency to trade off against others. Bill and his team treated them as part of the whole. After all, they were all potential customers—and company ambassadors as well. So out of those discussions came the idea of including them in the service pin program. Theirs would be the same design as the employee pin, but in silver.
>
> All pensioners received service award pins. The service award pin was a small gesture showing that the company appreciated pensioners and their contributions to the company.
>
> Judy and Bill were not sure how the pensioners would feel about the pin, since it had the AT&T logo on it and most of them had not worked for AT&T Canada. It turned out that the pensioners were very pleased to receive their pins and were proud that they had the AT&T brand on them. They felt valued by the company. It was a small token of recognition for their long service

that they could show to their friends and family.

Reflecting on how something of such low financial cost could have such a strong impact on people, Judy observed, "It was a simple thing to do. Some of the letters that Bill and I received were incredible, letters from long-service employees who had been harboring this bitterness for a number of years about how they had been asked to leave. It was all washed away by the presentation of this pin that from a monetary perspective was relatively low cost." While the traditional approach would have been to ignore pensioners, instead they had done something for them (at relatively low cost) that could help build greater respect for and loyalty to the company amongst this small but important group.

Evaluating and Developing Leaders. At the outset, Bill spent considerable time defining and discussing what he wanted from leaders. "We did that with the entire team. We sat down and defined what we expected of ourselves and from other leaders in this company. And we evaluated each other. It was very detailed. It took time—I took people off the job for a day or so to define the leadership requirements, measure ourselves, and provide feedback and coaching."

Bill and the senior team evaluated all of the top leaders, defined as at the level of "director" and above, essentially the top one hundred people of the company. High performers were those demonstrating desired leadership practices as defined by their list of leadership characteristics. Then the company provided leadership training to over 450 leaders—out of a company of less than three thousand!

Organization Structure. Then the PDR tackled the company's organization structure—how work gets done.

They started with Bill and his management team, defining what accountability each person had, including where one person's accountability started and ended vis-à-vis that of the other top executives. This included each of the top executives. One objective was to develop clarity. Another was to reduce or eliminate any overlap of responsibilities.

Once these accountabilities were defined, they used them as a guide to make sure that the lower level structures were lined up appropriately.

AT&T Canada LDS Dimensions of Leadership

(Note: The list also included "Key Behaviors" associated with each dimension.)

A. Managing Interpersonal Relationships

1) Energizing & Empowering Others
   The ability to energize employees, to maintain own energy and enthusiasm, and to act as a role model for others.
2) Building & Managing Teams
   The ability to organize, gain the involvement of, and manage diverse work groups and/or taskforces to accomplish specific project or unit goals.
3) Interpersonal Flexibility
   The ability to adapt behavior to different people and situations, while recognizing and addressing political and interpersonal sensitivities.

B. Achieving Business Results

1) Planning & Implementing
   The ability to anticipate resource needs, and then lay out priorities, and shape activities to meet objectives.
2) Decision Making
   The ability to know when and what decisions should be made and make several decisions simultaneously in a fast-paced, rapidly changing environment.
3) Breadth of Understanding
   The ability to critically evaluate information and to anticipate and understand the implications of decisions and actions on organizational components and people.
4) Business Knowledge
   The ability to appreciate the technical nature of the business, as well as how a particular function relates to that industry and the competition.
5) Business Results
   The ability to achieve business results while focusing on quality, customer satisfaction and profitability.

C. Influencing Others and Building Information Networks

1) Building Information Networks
   The ability to identify and obtain needed information by asking the appropriate questions and effectively utilizing information networks.
2) Influencing Others
   The ability to communicate persuasively orally and in written form to individuals and groups.

Retention. The Systems Department (reporting to the chief operating officer) was crucial to the company's revival. New business systems, especially related to the customer, were critical determinants of the company's ability to win back lost customers and retain current customers. In other words, the company needed to attract and retain good systems people.

The Systems organization was made up mostly of people who were new to the company and who worked in a different world. With their bouncing around to systems work wherever and whenever they wanted, they functioned similarly to independent contractors.

The executive team put their minds around the challenge this behavior posed in a series of PDR sessions. The team developed programs designed to retain systems people. In addition to making it attractive for them to stay, through such incentives as money and training, they also evaluated supervisors on whether their people stayed at the company.

Year Three: 1998

By the end of 1997 the company had begun to grow. They were meeting their plans, cutting expenses, and cutting losses. Everybody felt good. They were starting to say, "We're humming."

Culture. In many companies, when things are finally humming, people want to nail down what seems to be working, institutionalize it, document best practices, teach everyone, and even create new jargon to capture their winning formula.

Bill had something very different in mind. "You know what we have to do now? We've got to change. We're so successful in what we're doing that we have to change it. The time to change is when we're successful. And if we don't drive this change and drive it now, nobody else will. It's not going to happen of its own accord. We're the leaders."

Bill cut to the chase. "I'm going to posit the culture that I think we want, and I'm going to ask you if this is what you think also. I want a culture in which we are continuously improving—and continuously learning. If you were to ask me what I want every single person in this company to feel in their heart, it's 'I come into work every single day, and I continuously improve my job, and I'm continuously learning and improving myself.' If they said to me that this was their culture, I think we would have a company that nobody could stop. Now if you guys want to argue with me, go ahead."

One of the other executives jumped in. "We've been working on quality. We've been working on customer value. And we've been working on development, putting a lot of people through training. Isn't this really all about continuous personal improvement as well? I think that we're already doing this."

"Yes," Bill replied. "We know that we're doing this, but if you're in the bowels of the company, you don't know that all these things are happening. Nobody's putting the pieces together for you. Nobody's saying, 'Here's why we're doing it.'"

"I want people to be proud to be a part of this company. They will be proud for several reasons: because we're doing something good and we do it honestly. And also because we keep improving ourselves. I want them to say, 'I'm growing personally and professionally. What more can I want?' That's my objective, and we've got to work together to get there. So what's missing? Well, we've got this great quality program—continuously improving—which is the continuous improvement program. Every day we walk in and we're trying to find a better way to do our job, to serve our customers better, to improve our processes. That's part number one."

Part Two is about continuously improving ourselves. Thus, out of this and subsequent meetings came the concept of the AT&T Canada University for continuous learning. Bill commissioned a team of people from HR to design it.

The AT&T Canada University for Continuous Learning

The university, a virtual organization, would have different schools headed by senior leaders of the company. The curriculum would include the core strategy, individual effectiveness, leadership, career planning, wellness, technology, and more. Some courses, including ethics, would be required.

Employees received a brochure telling them that an AT&T Canada University was in the works. "You will be able to train yourself—online. You can sign up for courses. You can get certification. We're going to be affiliated with outside universities. We're going to have teaching in all the disciplines that you need to improve yourself personally and professionally."

Late in 1998, management introduced the university. Everybody received a card signed by Bill that conveyed the message, "You are not just an employee of AT&T Canada, you are a member of and a lifelong student at AT&T Canada University. How old you are or what your job is doesn't matter. As long as you are part of this company, you are always going to learn. Our concept is continuous improvement and continuous learning."

Succession planning. The PDR turned to succession planning as well. There had been very little turnover, almost too little. They developed a succession planning process, and the management development program to support it.

The succession planning started by addressing the direct reports to Bill and then expanded to the next level down, with a few additional highly critical positions below that.

They placed high emphasis on succession from within. The predecessor company had a long-time philosophy of not investing in people development but rather hiring from the outside when they needed it. Judy observed, "We made a conscious decision, wherever possible, that we would promote leaders from within. This was our one way to counter the retention challenge we had from companies that were publicly traded or could make the promise of becoming publicly traded. Recruiters wondered why we didn't use them, but our succession planning—and our management development program—reduced the need to do so."

Doing succession planning not only served the company, but also showed people that the company would assist them in their career objectives by promoting from within. For example, they helped a regulatory person move into a senior sales role. She had the right leadership characteristics to go into the sales organization, so management facilitated that move.

A President's Club for Everyone

George Harvey, president of the Commercial Business unit, approached Bill to propose a reinstitution of the President's Club, a recognition event for star salespeople. Bill said, "Fine. Take it to the PDR!" George then presented his proposal to his peer executives for discussion:

"Salespeople," he began, "like us to send them to the Bahamas if they're the top salespeople. The cost-cutting axe did away with that during the financial crisis years. We were going to have it last year. We had announced it, but then we had to cancel it. It was just a terribly demoralizing thing for the salespeople."

The manager of customer service said, "I don't want that. My people are going to get upset by it." In fact, most of the rest of the company had been saying, "Why are these fat cat salespeople going down to these fancy places?"

George responded, "We really *do* need this event to motivate our salespeople. To motivate and keep them, we need to provide recognition in addition to money. Even though the finance people and the customer service people don't understand it, we've got to do it. Salespeople are different. We've already lost some excellent salespeople, and we're going to lose more to other companies who do this."

The discussion went back and forth. Should they or should they not hold a recognition event for salespeople? What would it do for the morale of the salespeople—and to the morale of people in other functions?

Eventually it was time to make a decision. Bill made the call. "We're bringing back the President's Club. But there's going to be a little wrinkle. Half the people who go to the President's Club are going to be salespeople, based on their sales performance as measured by their sales numbers. The other half will be support people, who will be nominated and chosen based on their performance as measured by how well they live the values of the company—values like caring, respect, and integrity.

This was just the start. To actually implement the idea, the PDR set up a special committee to select those who would participate in the President's Club. The company now had a President's Club that was *for the whole company*, held in Cabo San Lucas.

Bill went to the club to reinforce the message that people and values were crucial to the company's success. But he also wanted to get to know these people better, so he could be even more in sync with the company's key people. In this way, he could be the orchestrator of a culture of deeply held and positively expressed values.

Building a Place Where People Can Bring Forth and Put All of Their Energies to Work

Running through all the work on the human dimension of the company was a deep respect for the incredible capabilities and contributions of people when management does the right things, and how everything that management does, in the end, contributes to either a great place to work or one that people want to leave.

Beliefs: People as Assets, Not Just Costs

Beliefs are the true foundation of any transformation effort. What we believe, we will actualize. If Unitel management believed that people were essentially a cost to be contained, then the HR function would have been primarily a people cost-control department. To become a true builder of people, HR and the company took on a radically different view of the people ingredient—that it is first and foremost an *asset*.

As an asset, it requires investment and maintenance or nurturing. That means that focus was placed as much on the capacity and output of that resource as on its cost. And it means that the company did not automatically pare down people when revenues were insufficient to pay for costs, but, rather, that it called on people to help rebuild the business.

Keeping the Humanity and Trust in Human Resource Policies

Carole Salomon, head of the residential business (Chapter 9), one day walked into the office of Anil Amlani, head of Strategic Planning. Seeing the picture of his son behind him, she asked Anil, "How's your son doing finding a job?"

"Not so well. He's working hard at it, but with no luck yet," he replied. Carole began thinking about how she had an opening that maybe Anil's son might fill. She wondered what the policy was about this. At Nabisco, her prior employer, the hiring of family members was discouraged. She dropped into Bill's office. "Would you have any trouble with my hiring Anil's son? What's our policy?"

Bill, the contrarian CEO, responded immediately, "I encourage it. What better reference can you get?"

So Carole hired Anil's son, who turned out to be an outstanding employee.

Several months later, Carole's own daughter visited her at the company. Bill came up to their lunch table and said to her daughter, "Why don't you join us?" So she did—and made sure she did her best.

A Culture that People Do Not Want to Leave

Judy McLeod never worked with recruiters when filling positions. She knew them all but could find people herself. When these recruiters frequently asked what AT&T Canada was doing that prevented them from recruiting *out* of the company, Judy replied, *"We're making a culture that people don't want to leave."*

CHAPTER 11

THE LEGACY

We have seen where the company was at the beginning of the turnaround. We have followed some of the key people as they addressed issues and worked together to bring about improvement in important dimensions of the company. In this chapter, we will look at the legacy of this turnaround effort, first in terms of the positioning of the company as an industry leader, and then in terms of its impact on the people who achieved this remarkable turnaround.

IMMEDIATE Impact: The Business Positioned as an Industry Leader

The company had been fading fast at the start of the three-year turnaround. At that time, it represented a small percentage of the industry and was declining further as customers and employees left. With losses of nearly a million dollars a day, it was about to go under.

The company not only survived, but started to thrive. Even just two years into the turnaround, a year before Bill Catucci retired from AT&T Canada, here is where the company stood on major business performance measures:

Quality

The Yankee Group, a technology consulting group, wrote about the company's transformation in quality in its November 1997 Canadian Market Strategies White Paper:

> "Under the guidance of Larry Hudson and his team, AT&T Canada met the AT&T Corp hurdles, and in fact exceeded the AT&T Corp, operating standards.... The network quality improvement was underscored recently by the endorsement of the Worldsource™ operations team—AT&T Canada Long Distance Services was accorded the fastest endorsement for its overall performance, and for its operations and provisioning practices of any company in the WorldPartners alliance."

They further noted that the company's network had been:

> "transformed... (having) passed the WorldPartners quality hurdles in six

months, while others have more typically taken a year for this feat."

Product Offering

In its 1997 report, the Gartner Group stated:

> *"Through 2002, AT&T Canada and Stentor will have the broadest, most advanced, feature-rich business telecom services in Canada....We advise all enterprises to include AT&T Canada in every telecom RFP, and large enterprises seeking the most sophisticated national services should turn to Stentor and AT&T Canada first."*

Employee Morale

As the theme of this book suggests, employee morale played a central role in generating superior financial performance. The Hay Group had conducted employee surveys even before Bill Catucci took over as CEO and continued during Bill's tenure. These externally generated reports are particularly instructive because they compare the company with the morale performance of five hundred other North American companies. The reports showed that:

- Overall, morale had risen from the bottom ten percent of those five hundred companies to the top five percent in just three years;
- The morale performance rose *during* the turnaround, not merely *after* the turnaround.
- The areas where the employee survey showed the most pronounced advantage over other companies were in such categories as their level of understanding of the company's strategy, their respect of their leaders, and their ability to learn and grow.

Financial Return

In just three years, Unitel/AT&T Canada LDS emerged from its state of trauma to become an industry leader. As early as August 1997, halfway through the three-year turnaround, the Gartner Group observed:

> *"AT&T Canada has gone through its greatest turmoil in the last two years. Its predecessor (Unitel) was near death in 1995, when it was losing almost CDN$1 million per day and two of its owners basically walked away from it. AT&T (U.S.) and three banks rescued the company, financing it until a turnaround could be mustered. That turnaround is approaching since AT&T*

134

> *Canada will achieve its goal of profitability in 1998 (0.8 probability). Much of this reversal can be attributed to improved service and support, improved morale and new staff at AT&T Canada, and a new leadership team."*

The report concluded with the observation:

> *"AT&T Canada has repaired past problems and will hold a strong position in the future Canadian telecom market."*

The "Bottom Line"

Indeed, on all levels, by the end of the third year of the turnaround (1998), the company had made enormous strides:

- a financially unstable company in 1995, it now had a strong balance sheet and solid financial backing;
- after losing nearly $1 million per day in 1995, its losses had been almost eliminated, putting it nearly in the black;
- a situation of warring owners with different agendas had become one with clear shareholder consensus on a strategy for not only surviving, but thriving;
- a company with low morale had become one with a highly dedicated and motivated workforce;
- a company focused only on survival had become a leading tele-communications provider with high-quality, state-of-the-art services, and was experiencing rapid growth.

Sustainable Growth and Profitability

Bill strove to put the company in a position where it could survive well into the future.

J.S. Darville, the Price Waterhouse engagement partner for AT&T Canada and national leader of the Price Waterhouse Entertainment Media and Communications practice in Canada, had been involved with the company since the early 1980s. He summed up the turnaround and Bill's leadership:

> *"I have found Bill to be a man of integrity with the ability to think strategically and execute tactically. When Bill took over the leadership of Unitel in January 1996, he was confronted with daunting challenges not only to turn the company around financially but also simply to deliver service. He had no leadership team and his fundamental product,*

the network, was poorly maintained and utilized. In only two years, I've witnessed an unbelievable transformation in AT&T LDS (Long Distance Services) under Bill's leadership. He has energized his workforce, is continuously rebuilding the network, has put in place operational and financial controls, has revitalized his marketing and sales organizations, and has personally established a first class reputation for LDS with major businesses in Canada.

"The turnaround that Bill Catucci has led at LDS is one of the most impressive I've seen not only because of the speed with which he has rebuilt every facet of the business, but also because the dynamic improvements he has made are enduring and mean that growth, productivity and profitability are sustainable."

The LASTING Impact

When people hear the story of what Bill and his team accomplished at Unitel/AT&T Canada LDS, some respond with, "Yes, but what happened *after* the CEO left?"—as if the turnaround was authentic and noteworthy *only* if the remarkable business results (and inspiring culture) continued *after* the CEO departed the company. If not, apparently in their minds, the CEO's achievements were somehow merely a mirage, temporary and thus not real and noteworthy.

What such a perspective overlooks, however, is that every new CEO creates her own management system and culture. And people in every organization are quick studies. They soon learn—often from stories that circulate throughout a company—how the new CEO operates and what kind of values that new CEO expects and rewards.

With that in mind, let us look at what happened at AT&T Canada *after* Bill left and a new CEO took over.

After the Turnaround

At the end of the turnaround, AT&T Canada bought out the banks which had recouped their former losses and enjoyed a substantial profit to become sole owner and expanded its product offerings to become a full-service provider of telecom services.

Then the Company sold off the residential business, which became part of Primus Telecommunications Group.

Next, they sold the rest of AT&T Canada Long Distance Services, oriented to the commercial market. This became Allstream Inc.

Though difficult to compare the company during Bill's leadership with the company after he left, it is clear that he and his team left a strong foundation of services and quality, market share, and brand image and organization on which subsequent management built in order to sell the company for several times what it was worth when Bill took the helm in early 1995.

ORGANIZATION: Building Lasting Strength

Major turnarounds are created sometimes at the cost of morale and organization strength. This turnaround, because it was largely driven through the human dimension, had a lasting positive impact on organization strength.

People

What happened at the people level after Bill left provides valuable insights about what can be changed permanently and what needs constant leadership to keep at high levels.

Judy McLeod had taken the HR director's job because, like Bill, she believed that the human resources function could and should play a key role in turning the company around. She observed:

"The impact was evident from the employee survey. We reached best-in-class levels. This bought us tremendous loyalty, which in turn translated into customer satisfaction.

"We could see the connection between employee satisfaction and customer satisfaction. We had impressive revenue growth [which tracked with employee satisfaction].

"Retention was tremendous. By the environment that we created, there was very low turnover in the management ranks. And this was at a time when IPOs beckoned to high performers throughout the industry. You could count on the fingers of one hand the number of people we lost whom we didn't want to lose."

Morale

Four years after the turnaround, Judy related what happened following Bill's departure:

"When we stepped out on our own, there was a vacuum. People mourned for a year.

"The next time we did an employee survey, the results were not nearly as good. But a lot was going on. We had merged five different operating businesses. The industry imploded. The whole business climate had changed.

"New leaders were saying we had to cut costs, which took us back to being focused on just a single dimension. We lost ground.

"But the union relationship remains strong even though executives have changed.

"The management system remains intact. We had to fight to keep that.

"The emphasis on quality remains strong. Even with all our changes, we retain a holistic approach to balancing the business.

"A lot of the Human Resource programs are better. In Bill's time we created a foundation. Bill started 'people friendly policies' and that emphasis remains.

"Gradually, morale levels dropped back somewhat, though the executives who remained worked at building and nurturing morale."

Culture

How does a CEO who creates a vibrant culture where people are honored and empowered to achieve new levels of development and performance ensure that the culture lives on after he or she leaves? The answer seems to be that he or she cannot. It is natural for incoming CEOs to want to create their own culture—and to be upset with those who cling to the old culture.

Yet there were aspects of the culture that did continue, even if not advocated by the new top management. Speaking over a year after Bill retired, Renato Discenza, head of Operations, said:

"It's amazing how many people are resilient because of the values we created. Why are they able to put up with the changes that have been introduced since Bill left better than most others would? I believe it has to do with the values they have, values of customer service and wanting to serve their people. You can throw a lot of changes at them, but there are certain principles in how they do their work that are deeper than the changes themselves. It's about the way they do their work."

INDIVIDUAL: Awakening and Invigorating Human Spirit

In Bill's view, although you cannot expect as a CEO to change the culture permanently, you can strive to open people's hearts and minds to what is possible, to what can be achieved by individuals, teams, and the company. And, it's not just about the outer dimension of what can be achieved, but also about the inner dimension of what it is possible to *be* as an individual, as a team, and as a company. This is about the values that will be manifest, no matter what the strategy, who the top management, or who the customer. And it is this inner dimension that can be lasting and provide an ongoing source of great business performance.

The Leadership Team

Bill often said that immediate business results are fleeting and fade with time and that the CEO's greatest lasting impact is on the people he or she leads. What kind of difference have you made in their lives? Have they been able to reach new levels of capability?

Members of Bill's leadership team reflected on their experience of working together:

George Harvey, president, Business Service Group:
"When Bill persuaded me to come out of semi-retirement, [I did it] with a certain amount of trepidation—after all, I had not reported to any single person for over seventeen years—always to a board, none of whom resided down the corridor from me! However, from day one, there was no concern. Bill was a class act and an outstanding individual to work with.

"In my thirty-eight years in business, I have never met or worked with an individual who had such a magnetic personality ...[and] the ability to turn even the most cynical employee into a loyal supporter."

Renato Discenza, head of Operations:
"I learned from Bill. He walks the talk. He worked at it every day. It wasn't just that he was a nice guy. He worked at analyzing himself and figuring out 'Where do I fall short?' He'd even ask people to criticize him. He'd say, 'I'm looking for examples of how I did not live up to this value.' He'd work on it by himself.

"Bill would get direct reports to come in and give him a review by asking, 'How did I do supporting you?'

"Because of this behavior, even the language changed. It used to be, 'I'm the VP of such and such.' It became, 'I support this department.' When I went to an outside seminar, people went around the table saying who they were. When I said, 'I'm Renato Discenza. I support Network Services,' people were surprised and confused. People had never heard this kind of language. Bill brought this in.

"As a leader, you support people. The leader is a servant. If you want to be a leader, it's not about power. It's about being willing to serve your troops! Figuring out what they need, equipping them with the tools, the knowledge, and the empowerment. That's the leadership job. This also means setting the right environment, giving the challenges, then letting them go and engage. You can't fight their fight for them. You just coordinate the battle."

Judy McLeod, senior VP, Human Resources:

"I have never worked for anyone before or since who made me (and many others) feel so valued and so important.

"It gave me a huge confidence boost in believing in myself, and I have been able to retain that."

Taking These Lessons to Other Companies

Bill Catucci, after retiring from Unitel/AT&T Canada LDS, accepted an offer to help lead the turnaround of Equifax, an Atlanta-based financial services company whose business performance had become stagnant. Could he pull off another dramatic turnaround, or was the one he just led merely a fluke? Would the leadership philosophy and management approaches he used in a Canadian company work in a U.S. company?

At Equifax, he used the same basic approach he did at AT&T Canada LDS, with a strong emphasis on creating and communicating a compelling mission and values, then building those into the company's decision making. He introduced the Balanced Scorecard and measured all the key dimensions of business performance he had at AT&T Canada, including measures of quality, customer satisfaction, and employee morale. And he introduced the Integrated Strategic Management System.

Within his three years as EVP at Equifax, during which he first led the domestic operations of Equifax and then its global operations, he once again led a successful effort to raise employee morale, quality, customer satisfaction, and financial performance. Market share rose, profit margins rose, and the company's market value rose by over $3 billion—this during a period (1999–2002) when the stock market was volatile.

Renato Discenza took his wisdom and experience to Bell Canada, where he has used the leadership lessons of the turnaround to bring about major improvements in performance. After each such turnaround or revitalization, the company has asked him to take on more responsibility, most recently to lead a division of Bell Canada with ten thousand employees, where he served until early 2008.

Judy McLeod became EVP of Customer Service at **Allstream** telecommunications, where she served until 2005.

Carole Salomon became president of **AllStream.**

Charlotte Daigle-Basque stayed on with the company. Her unit became part of Primus, and she worked there until they closed it down. She later opened a restaurant in Edmunston, New Brunswick, and also became a service delivery director for Teletech, a start up company to help create jobs in the area.

Individual Employees—An Inner Transformation

How did the three-year turnaround affect employees, people down in the ranks who did not work in the senior management team but who responded to the call by management to help turn the company around?

When he announced his retirement, Bill was flooded with cards and emails from hundreds of employees thanking him for his leadership and sharing what the three years had meant to them and how it had changed them. Though their comments of course focused on Bill and his leadership, their cards and emails also showed what kind of lasting changes in outlook, in spirit, and in motivation took place within these people. Here are just a few messages, each from a different person:

> *It was the way that you led this company that touched me the most....*
> *It amazed me the way you instilled a positive attitude and environment*
> *throughout the entire company, the way your vision spread throughout the*

ranks, and most importantly, how you genuinely expressed care and respect for all your employees.

When I first started here as a residential customer service agent, you came to visit us in one of our training classes to welcome us and share your vision for this company. By the end of your address, we could hardly wait to get out there and start working. You filled us with so much enthusiasm and excitement! We were so pleased that you had taken the time to come and see us, to talk and to listen.

Thank you for giving so much of yourself to everyone in this company. You made us feel important, you made us feel confident and you made us feel proud. We in turn have been so proud of you! As with many others, I plan to continue to do everything I can to make this company a success.

You taught me about family balance at our sales kickoff, which left me with a lasting lesson about priorities. It was the first time I had personally heard an executive speak about family in an open forum. Having just returned from maternity leave, it helped me maintain a harmony that I will always strive to keep in my life.

Until I came to AT&T Canada and worked for you and your company, I felt that all anyone cared about was the bottom line.

You have really had a personal effect on me and made me proud to work here.... I have been a face in the crowd, but your words always stayed with me.

As I listened to you this morning over the teleconference [announcing his retirement], a number of thoughts, events, and memories crossed my mind.... The main thing that struck me was that this man wishing us the best in this new chapter of our corporate life was not only the best CEO that I ever experienced in any company I worked for, but most importantly, he was a friend, a confidant, a mentor, and an inspiration for many of us. You have made us better persons both professionally and personally.

You joined us at a time of adversity and you gave us hope. Your strengths became our strengths. You turned this into a fun place to work again.

Thank you for teaching me to believe—not only in myself—but in the "vision."

We will continue to use the lessons we have learned under your guidance and the experiences we have gained to continue on the odyssey which you have created.... Thank you from the heart.

One person wrote, "*Your encouragement helped me believe that if I don't quit and I work hard, I can achieve anything I dream of in life*"— then added this poem:

I'll miss you in my heart,
I'll remember you in my head.
Your beautiful words of encouragement,
I'll live everything you said.

Expanding the Definition of Success

In the end, the transformation of Unitel/AT&T Canada was powered by an inner transformation of beliefs, of vision, of desires, of courage, and of commitment. With this transformation, the Energies of Head, Hands, Emotions, Heart and Will all came together to create an uncommon turnaround—both at an inner human level—and an outer business level.

It also triggered a rethinking of, and expansion of, participants' views of success. In their letters of appreciation to Bill, several employees sent the same poem, "Success," attributed to Ralph Waldo Emerson:

"To laugh often and much;
to win the respect of intelligent people
and the affection of children;
to earn the appreciation of honest critics
and endure the betrayal of false friends;
to appreciate beauty, to find the best in others;

to leave the world a bit better,

whether by a healthy child,

a garden patch

or a redeemed social condition;

to know even one life has breathed easier

because you have lived.

this is to have succeeded."

Years after the turnaround, people throughout the company still gather to reminisce and stay connected with each other. Reflecting on this phenomenon, Judy McLeod observed in early 2006, nearly seven years after the turnaround, *"It is unusual for people who leave a company to get back together for a reunion. In the case of AT&T Canada people getting together, I think it's because people invested so much of themselves in the company. Just this past October, two hundred people attended such a reunion in Toronto."*

PART III

ORIGINS OF A NEW CORPORATION

CHAPTER 12

A HUMAN ECONOMICS

> "...To make the connection between people and profits, organizations are going to have to *think* a little differently and *manage* a lot differently than many of their competitors. ...In the end, making the connection between people and profits entails confronting how we think about work, organizations, and the people in them." (emphasis added)
>
> —Jeffrey Pfeffer, *The Human Equation: Building Profits by Putting People First*, 1998

How did the management and employees of Unitel/AT&T Canada LDS bring off this remarkable turnaround? The *actions* that they took to transform the company were not particularly earth-shattering or novel. Others have taken similar actions but have not necessarily succeeded. What, then, made this turnaround so successful?

To discover the answer we need first to look at the ways in which Bill Cattuci and his team did (to use Pfeffer's language above) "think a little differently." This different thinking started with a fundamentally different view of the underlying economics of business—the subject of this chapter. In subsequent chapters, we'll translate that thinking into a business model and leadership that represents a different way of "managing."

ECONOMIC REALITY: Define It Right, Then Operate Within It

Whether conscious or unexamined, in all companies leaders and employees alike hold beliefs about how the business world operates, what we call the "real world." They shape their views of what is possible, what strategies they need to succeed, their interpretation of events, etc., to fit that "real world." This reality we will call the underlying "economic reality of business."

Thus, even while companies and their leaders focus on the specifics of their industry, its markets and customers, its competitive forces, and the strategies to succeed in that particular mix of ingredients, there is an underlying "economic reality of business" within which these forces play out.

Getting the "thinking" right about this economic reality of business is essential to leaders and their companies' success.

Two primary views of that underlying economic reality exist. One is a Material-centered Economics that stems from our industrial past, which puts material (and financial) resources at the center of the economic business model. The second is a more recent and still emerging one—a Human-centered Economics, which puts the human being (and organization) at the center of the economic business model.

A Material Economic Reality

Economics is the study and science of serving human needs, individually and collectively, by taking scarce resources and converting them into the products and services that best serve those human needs.

Until the late twentieth century, that meant mostly serving the material needs of people (and of other companies) through material products and services.

In a Material Economic reality, the purpose of business is to convert raw (physical) materials into more valuable physical goods designed to satisfy our material needs, initially for food, clothing, shelter, and transportation and allied services, and more recently for a growing array of material goods.

The management methods developed within a Material Economic view of reality focus on the material dimension of the company. And this Material Economics view of reality extends beyond just industrial companies, for the thinking of Material Economics, especially about organizations and leadership, is so ingrained that it runs through many companies that are not part of the industrial segment of the economy.

A company's key resources in the Material Economics reality are raw physical materials, production equipment, and facilities—material assets purchased with financial capital. The primary human ingredient is physical labor, treated as a cost of production along with the costs of raw materials.

Measures of performance are designed primarily to measure the flow of materials and products and purchase and sales transactions. Profit margins and return on physical assets and financial investment are the criteria of success.

To succeed in a Material Economy, companies adopt strategies such as: creating economies of scale (so that the considerable fixed costs of plant and

Economic Reality: Two Versions
And the Business Model for Each

The Underlying Economics	**Material** Economics Attributes	**Human** Economics Attributes
Purpose of economic activity	Provide needed <u>products</u> or <u>materials</u> to consumers and other companies	Serve <u>human needs</u> and <u>aspirations</u> – material and nonmaterial or support other companies in doing same
Typical Industries	Materials-based companies	Knowledge-based and relationship-based companies
Why People Work	<u>Physical Survival</u> & Material well being	<u>Self-actualization</u> & Happiness and Fulfillment
Primary Resources Companies use	<u>Material Assets</u> Physical: Equipment, Materials Financial: for startup and expansion	<u>Human Beings</u> Their Talents and Energies - and Character and Relationships
Human Ingredient	Physical labor: Getting work done	....Also Mind & Spirit
Driver of Wealth Creation	**Financial Capital**	**Human Capital**
The Resulting Business Model		
The Corporation as	A **Material Entity**: Facilities, Products, Raw Materials & Working Capital	A **Human Entity**: Skills, Experience & Character And the Relationships of People
Objective	Maximize profitability of operations and Return to Shareholders	Serve multiple stakeholders: Employees, Customers, Shareholders & Community
Business Strategy	Create economies of scale, minimize costs, and optimize operations	Hire people with talent and character, and inspire them to succeed
Human Ingredient	...a Cost-based **Resource** ∞ **Expensed** ∞ **Expendable** People are not on the Balance Sheet	...the **Core** of the Business ∞ **An Asset** ∞ **Invested in** Truly "our most valuable asset"
Money is....	The Key Resource: It buys the Material Resources we need	One of several resources "Purchasable" with Human Capital
Measure of Success	Earnings Growth and Return on **Financial Capital**	Earnings Growth and Return on **Human Capital**

equipment are spread over a large volume of product), becoming the low-cost producer by acquiring raw materials and human labor at the lowest possible cost, and by optimizing operations (by extracting the most from available resources, minimizing down-time and errors, and increasing efficiency). In each case, management strives to operate a "tight ship" or "well-oiled machine" by using disciplined planning and control techniques.

Thus, when managements that function from a Material Economics mindset shape a turnaround strategy, they naturally focus on slashing operating costs (including people) and such so-called nonoperating costs (like R&D and training) and postponing pay raises and investments in physical and technological improvements, all to shore up cash flow. This is often called becoming "lean and mean." The assumption is that revenue will continue on and that the immediate task is to reduce costs; presto, profits rise. The resulting increase in profit margins combined with reduced cash outflow (for such things as more equipment and inventories or for "postponable" expenses), then yield needed positive cash flow to shore up the balance sheet.

All this thinking is accurate from a static accounting standpoint. In fact, reported profits may rise—temporarily. But that does not necessarily mean that they have created a sustainable business turnaround. In part, this is because those cuts in costs (and people) can weaken a company, which makes it more difficult to maintain those revenues that we have assumed will continue on into the future.† It's also because the Material Economics thinking misses such a powerful ingredient—people.

A Human Economics Reality

A Human Economics mindset puts the human being at the core of the business. The key resource in this view of reality is people, not materials and financial resources. The material dimension in this mindset is not ignored; it is still seen as an important ingredient that people use to create business success. And the material dimension provides an important *measure* of success. You need profitability to stay in business, of course. But that profitability, in a Human Economics mindset, comes from what you do with the people of the business.

†See the author's article "Rebuilding the Human Spirit after Downsizing" PIMA (Paper Industry Management Association) (December 1996). The journal described this article thus: "While downsizing has meant improved financial returns for many companies, it has shaken employee morale and commitment. In the aftermath, what can be done to rebuild the human dimension?"

Business—seen through the eyes of Human Economics thinking—is about the flow not merely of materials and finance but first and foremost of *human energy* and talent through the organization. Management's job, then, in a Human Economics reality is to unleash that energy flow and guide it toward the company's objectives.

Since Human Economic thinking sees the human resource as the key resource that drives the success of the business, it follows that in this reality any major turnaround or revitalization effort must focus first and foremost on revitalizing and strengthening that human resource and helping it to lift the company out of the depths.

That in a nutshell is what the AT&T Canada turnaround was all about. Sure, management took actions to reduce costs and to manage cash flow. But the beginning of this turnaround consisted not so much of (continued) traditional belt-tightening, but rather of refinancing the company to infuse it with more financial capital so that it could invest in strengthening the company's assets.

In addition to strengthening the company's telecommunications network to improve its performance, it also included actions to strengthen and empower the human asset. In what might seem like the wrong move to a Material Economics thinker, the self-described "contrarian" leader Catucci, instead of cutting back on the human resource, actually *increased* the "investment" (measured as "costs" by traditional accounting) in the human dimension of the business. Recall these investments of both time and money:

- The nearly half million dollars that the company paid early in the form of $175 checks to each employee as a symbol of appreciation of their service and a symbol of what they would accomplish together;
- Reinstating the President's Club (which had been curtailed to save costs) with two hundred people being honored at a retreat at an upscale resort;
- Service pins for employees and retirees;
- A leadership development program for the company's top leaders, with outside consulting support;
- Hay Group Employee morale surveys and planning and action specifically aimed at raising morale;
- Establishing an AT&T Canada University for life-learning for its employees.

Seen through the eyes of a Material Economics thinker, these actions would be crazy because (from a traditional accounting approach) they reduce reported profits even further—a dangerous move for a company whose losses had reached one million dollars per day! Yet they were solidly logical from a Human Economics mindset (made possible because of the new infusion of additional financial capital). Seen through the eyes of a Human Economics thinker like Bill Catucci, this strategy and related actions were the logical (though seemingly "contrarian" to conventional wisdom) path to revitalizing the company.

As Catucci put it, reflecting on the company's turnaround,

> *"It's a story about how a company can be turned around, if you focus on what's important and you involve people in the right way. In the end, it's a story about the turnaround of* people, *because ultimately the people* are *the company."*

Employing Human Economics Thinking

The thinking behind all this behavior is a belief in the power of a Human-centered Economics in which investments in the human resource—both financial investment and the psychic investment through a people-centered management philosophy—pays off several-fold as inspired, uplifted, and empowered people create what others might call miraculous results.

Exploring this Human-centered Economic mindset, we see several ways this approach differs from the traditional Material Economics thinking that many managements still draw on when attempting to grow companies and raise profitability.

In a world of human economics, business goes beyond meeting merely the basic needs of consumers for physical survival. Abraham Maslow's "hierarchy of needs" is useful in this context because it explains motivation, which aims to meet certain unfulfilled needs. As our physical survival becomes less and less of an issue, for example, other needs become operative. Social needs follow physical needs: people need to feel that they belong and are accepted, and they need to have self-esteem. Then there are needs for personal growth. People need to learn, explore, and create; and they need to connect with nature and find beauty. Ultimately, they seek self-actualization, the opportunity to develop themselves and achieve fulfillment from the work itself.

The Evolution of Human Capital

The rise in Human Economic thinking is powered in part by the evolution of the concept of Human Capital. This evolution is still underway, as we'll see later in this chapter.

"Capital" originally meant financial capital. In an industrial world, it took massive amounts of this (financial) capital to build companies—to put up buildings, buy equipment, purchase raw materials, and to finance the growth of the company (funding its working capital of products, raw materials, and accounts receivable from customers). Furthermore, since it typically took some time before a new company reached a point where its sales revenues exceeded its expenses, the funds required to finance an industrial company were essential and hence viewed as the driver of the wealth creation process. Even after a company achieved profitable operations and sought to grow, this process required more financial capital—more equipment and more working capital to fund that growth.

The concept of Human Capital emerged in the mid twentieth century as a new revolutionary concept—the idea that the human resource was not just a cost of doing business but actually a form of "capital" that a company needed to succeed along with financial capital. Gary Becker, a Nobel laureate in economics who published the book *Human Capital* in 1964, actually hesitated to use the term *human capital* because it sounded demeaning and exploitive on the surface. This radical way of thinking about the people ingredient of business has helped CEOs conceptualize their companies more accurately than the older Material Economics' concept of people as merely a "factor of production."

A second step in the evolving understanding of the role of Human Capital in business was the suggestion that it is no longer financial capital (and its major use, physical capital), but rather Human Capital that is the true driver of the wealth creation process. Milton Friedman, another Nobel Laureate economist, put it this way in his 1981 book *Free to Choose:*

> "The accumulation of physical capital... has played an essential role in economic growth. But the accumulation of human capital—in the form of increased knowledge and skills and improved health and longevity—has also played an essential role. And the two have reinforced one another.... Both physical and human capital must be cared for and replaced. That is even more difficult and costly for

human than for physical capital—a major reason why the return to human capital has risen so much more rapidly than the return to physical capital."

Thus the business model has changed from a time of Material Economics, in which:

- It was financial capital that drove the wealth creation process through the purchase of plant and equipment and the financing of material inventories.
- The human ingredient, primarily labor, was expensed and expendable.
- People were seen as—and accounted and managed as—a "commodity."

In a time of Human Economics:

- It is human capital that drives the wealth creation process.
- Financial capital is "purchased" by companies with strong Human Capital.
- The "commodity" is financial capital.

Thus Human Capital becomes the driver of the wealth creation process in the Human Economics reality—and thus the key resource. Financial capital, on the other hand, becomes just one of many resources that the company needs to succeed, and in fact can be "bought" by companies with great Human Capital.

In companies that function in a human economics reality, financial capital loses its role as the primary driver of wealth creation and becomes a commodity. Human capital now drives the wealth creation process, and companies with strong Human Capital can purchase financial capital (versus the reverse, which is the case in a world of Material Economics).

MANAGING in a Human Economics Reality

Each of the two views of economic reality calls for different management approaches.

Managers operating in a Material Economics mindset logically focus on the physical dimension and seek to optimize these *outer* forms—the products, the right markets, the right work flow—and to take the right actions, for example seeking to employ so-called best practices. "Getting it right" in a Material Economics world means essentially right actions resulting in zero defects, and doing it *right* the first time.

Management Principles
For Each Economic Reality

	Management Principles For Operating within an Economic Reality of...	
	Material Economics	**Human Economics**
Management Focus:	**Right Outer Forms** • *Right products, right production processes, right markets, etc.*	**Right Inner Energies** • *Right employees – right skills, but also right attitude & energy*
Getting it "Right"	**Right (Efficient) Action** • *"Best practices"* • *"Zero defects"*	**Right (Effective) Relationships** • *"Best Values"* • *Positive energy flow*
The Management Imperative: Assure….	Efficient **FLOW** of *Materials* from raw materials to finished products to capitalize on production efficiency	Effective **FLOW** of *Information & Human Energy* to capitalize on ideas and relationships
Human Needs	**Physical Survival & Material Wealth** • *Food, Clothing, Shelter – 1900* • *The "Good Life" – 2000* • *Scarcity Mentality*	**Nonmaterial Goals & Wellbeing** • *Purpose & Meaning* • *Self-actualization* • *Making a difference*
The Organization as	A well-oiled "machine" Everyone in it a "cog"	A Living Organism Everyone a key part of the Whole
Key Roles of Management	• Keep the "machine" running smoothly and product flowing • Maximize efficiency	• Keep human energies flowing • Inspire with higher purpose • Manage interrelationships
The Management System	• Focuses on & Optimizes *Parts* • Builds culture of efficiency • Finds & eliminates problems • Cuts costs • Controls decisions and actions	• Focuses on the *Whole* • Builds culture of high purpose and ethical values • Stimulates innovation • Builds collaboration & respect
Key Performance Measures	**Transactions** & their profitability • *Production transactions*	**Relationships** & their profitability • *Customer satisfaction*

	• *Sales transactions*
	• *Product line profit margins*
	• *Return on financial investment*
	   e.g., ROA, (Return on Assets)
		• *Employee morale & motivation*
		• *Collaboration & creativity*
		• *Return on human investment*
		   e.g., ROHC
		   (Return on Human Capital)

Managers operating in a Human Economics mindset focus on the knowledge and inner energies that people bring to work. They seek to optimize the inner dimension, i.e. human energies, for example, hiring for attitude not just knowledge and experience. They work at encouraging and nurturing the network of human relationships that make up the company.

Another way to understand the difference between these two economic mindsets is to think of a business in terms of not just its assets and resources, but in terms of flow. What flow do leaders manage in each economic reality? In a Material Economic reality, managers see their job as managing the efficient flow of materials and seek to optimize that flow. Managers in a Human Economic reality, on the other hand, see their job as managing the effective flow of human energy and talent and seek to stimulate and optimize that flow.

Each economic mindset sees and acts on a different view of human needs. In a Material Economic reality, human needs have historically been mostly about physical survival. A hundred years ago, nearly all personal income was spent on the basics—food, clothing, and shelter. More recently, motivation has been increasingly more about material well-being—"The Good Life."

In a Human Economic reality, people are motivated by nonmaterial needs and goals as well, such as self-realization. (More about this in the next chapter.)

Managers in a Material Economics world see the organization as a kind of machine, with every person being a cog in that machine. Their objective is to keep that organizational machine running smoothly. Managers in a Human Economics world see the organization more as a network of human energies and concentrate on keeping human energies flowing creatively and inspiring people.

Companies with a Material Economics mindset create management systems that focus on the companies' various parts, that manage efficiency, and that seek to find, even anticipate, problems and correct (or prevent) them, with highly developed controls to make sure people follow prescribed behavior.

Companies with a Human Economics mindset, conversely, see and optimize the whole—they see the interconnections, not just the parts. They concentrate on inspiring people with a compelling corporate purpose and ethical values. They build the company's culture, one of collaboration and mutual respect.

The performance measures that management tracks and uses to manage the business also differ. The company rooted in Material Economics measures material transactions and material and financial assets. The company rooted in Human Economics measures the strength of its human relationships through customer satisfaction and employee morale surveys.

Over the years, as the human dimension of companies has started playing an increasingly central role, a Human Economics mindset has become ever more needed and effective. Yet even so, most businesses have a role for both Material Economic thinking and Human Economic thinking. The challenge for managers today is to determine the balance between the two ways of thinking—to choose consciously in which mindset to operate.

THREE ECONOMIC AGES

As the economy has evolved, the Human Economics perspective has become increasingly relevant and helpful. Let's look at the role of the human dimension in three economic ages—the historical Industrial Age, the current Information Age, and an emerging Relationship Age.

In the twentieth century, we witnessed the gradual decline of the Industrial Age and flowering of the Information Age. The Relationship Age has recently emerged and, together with the Information Age, represents the era of human economics.

Each age is distinguished by dominant tendencies, not clear demarcations. Companies operating in the Industrial Age, for example, may be involved in manufacturing but approach it with the mindset of the Information Age, using technology to innovate and to control material flow, equipment scheduling, and human activity. Likewise, firms that operate in the Information Age may employ the mindset of the Relationship Age to build and capitalize on networks of people that generate business. Conversely, even companies operating in the Relationship Age must incorporate Information Age–thinking to assure innovation and technological progress and Industrial Age–thinking to manage its physical and financial resources, but not lose site of the greater importance of the network of human relationships that powers the business.

Similarly, sources of competitive advantage build upon one another and differ only in emphasis among the economic ages. Financial capital (and the physical assets which it purchases) serves as the primary driver of business success in the Industrial Age. In the Information Age, it is Intellectual Capital (and the application of technology) that is the driver, while Spiritual Capital (and the networks of human relationships it spawns) is the principal driver of success in the Relationship Age.

By the time the AT&T Canada LDS turnaround was well underway, the organization was making progress on the performance measures from each age, tapping the minds of employees to improve quality (tapping the fruits of the Information Age) and achieving higher profit margins on products and services (an Industrial Age measure), using progress on Relationship Age issues of employee morale and collaboration (as measured by the Hay Group employee survey).

Let's look closely at each age to see its characteristics and the economic and management principles of each.

Industrial Age

Industrial Age companies extract natural resources and/or use raw materials to create material products. These are the companies that drove the U.S. economy until just a few decades ago; for example, General Motors, U.S. Steel, Union Pacific Railroad, Esso (now Exxon-Mobil), DuPont, and many others founded in the nineteenth and early to mid twentieth centuries.

Large amounts of financial capital are needed to create these companies. Manufacturing facilities, materials, and labor must be funded before there can be customers or revenue; and company growth also requires the infusion of financial capital. The company goal is to maximize the return on this financial investment, which means that the primary management tools are financial and physical measures and processes, as well. Variables such as sales margins, turnover ratios, output per machine and per "man-hour," and return on capital investment are the indicators of performance.

Management's challenge is to maximize productivity by optimizing the flow of materials from acquisition to processing to distribution. Companies need employees to use their physical strength and manual dexterity to perform the work that keeps the flow moving but treat them as expenses—and expendable.

The human organization is seen as a "machine" with each person like a cog in that machine (within a box on an organization chart). The role of people is primarily physical labor, and even for those in staff jobs, it's about getting work organized and done—from inbox to outbox. The charge to people is to "Work Harder."

Even though much of the U.S. economy has moved beyond the

Three Economic Ages
And How to Succeed in Each

AGES & their Worldview	Primary Form of CAPITAL	Core PROCESS	HUMAN Dimension	LEADER'S Role
INDUSTRIAL Age 19th & Early 20th Century Traditional Capitalism: ***Financial Capital*** as the source of wealth	**MATERIAL Capital** Money Physical Assets Natural Resources	Flow of MATTER & Physical Energy Industries: Manufacturing, transportation, finance, etc.	The **Organization** as a "Well-oiled Machine" **Manual Laborers** To Succeed: **Work Harder**	**Leader** extracts physical energy and prevents errors <u>Business Strategy</u> Competitive advantage via operational efficiency & economies of scale
INFORMATION Age Late 20th Century Intellectual Capitalism: ***Information & Technology*** as the source of wealth	**INTELLECTUAL Capital** Information Knowledge Technology Processes & Systems	Flow of INFORMATION & Mental Energy Industries: Electronics, professional services, medical, etc.	The **Learning Organization** **Knowledge Workers** To Succeed: **Work Smarter**	**Leader** stimulates mental activity & creativity <u>Business Strategy</u> Competitive advantage via rapid commercialization of ideas & technology
RELATIONSHIP Age Emerging Spiritual Capitalism: ***Human Spirit*** as the source of wealth	**SPIRITUAL Capital** Purpose & Will Wisdom & Heart Emotional Energy	Flow of Human SPIRIT All Industries that depend on human relationships	The **NOBLE ENTERPRISE** **Light Workers** To Succeed: **Work with Purpose & Passion**	**Noble Leader** inspires people to bring their whole selves to work in service to the highest purpose. <u>Business Strategy</u> Competitive advantage via passionate people and energized relationships

A Law Firm Discovers the Power of Client Relationships

A small law firm asked me to help them become more profitable. In the view of the four partners, there were two main ingredients in the profit equation of their firm: legal expertise (to attract clients and provide value to them) and office efficiency (to get the work done efficiently). They felt justifiably confident about the first variable because their expertise in employment law was widely respected, and they regularly received referrals from other law firms, even far from their office. They also told me their success rate was high, which attracted even more business and drove the growth of the firm. The office efficiency factor affected the profitability of each case, and they felt it could stand improvement, so they asked me to focus on ways to improve staff productivity. After interviewing the partners and staff, I met with the partners to share my observations about the avenue to greater success.

I suggested that they consider a third factor in their conceptual model of their firm—that of their relationships with clients. After describing how important such relationships can be to success—in creating customer goodwill, supporting higher fee levels, and stimulating referrals—I asked them first to estimate the relative importance of each factor. Their chart looked like this:

Then I asked them to assess the strength of each factor in their firm by shading the

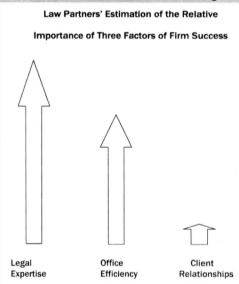

Law Partners' Estimation of the Relative Importance of Three Factors of Firm Success

Legal Expertise | Office Efficiency | Client Relationships

bar up to the percentage of perfection that they felt they had achieved. For the first bar, legal expertise, they filled it nearly all in. The bar for office efficiency, they filled in only part way, and the client relationships bar was mostly filled in.

Then I told them a story about one of their clients and her experience with the firm. It was actually a positive story as far as client relationships go and was one I had heard from several people in the firm, but this time, I asked them to listen to the story in terms of the three profitability factors we had put up on the flip chart.

The client had brought a workplace sexual harassment case to the firm. While the firm handled her case, one of its paralegals took it upon herself to create a supportive relationship with the client, calling her periodically, not just to tell her where the case was, but also to connect and be there for the woman.

The firm lost her case. End of story? No. The woman felt so well taken care of (despite the firm not winning her case) that she referred several other people who had similar cases to the firm. This turned out to be worth $600,000 in legal fees!

The partners knew the story but, probably because they were so focused on their legal expertise, had not incorporated it into their model of business success. They had seen the story as an interesting footnote, an aberration from their stellar legal track record. After all, they had "failed" in winning the case. Standing back from their firm, looking at the drivers of success, and considering the strategic importance of the story, they began to shift their economic model from merely an Information Age one (in which their legal expertise was the primary driver of success) to a Relationship Age model, in which relationships with clients and how they are treated become an important driver of success.

Industrial Age, companies and managers retain, in almost a hard-wired fashion, the beliefs about what's needed to be successful. Managers seek to make their mark by demanding efficiency—and zero defects—not only in the output of the company, but in the functioning of the human organization. This is basically a transference of the thinking about what management wants from machines directly to what they want from people.

Information Age

Information Age companies are built with—and sell—technology and information-based products and services. These companies have redefined the human ingredient, in the process transforming the world of work and becoming a powerful economic force. At one end of the spectrum are the Googles and Microsofts; at the other end, the law firm or medical clinic down the street. In between are thousands of ventures that operate within the context of the Information Age, employing knowledge workers and creating and/or using Intellectual Capital to serve customers who need this component to add value for their customer.

These companies manage the flow of ideas and technologies from conception to development to testing to full commercialization. Competitive advantage lies in coupling superior technology and knowledge with fast time-to-market capabilities. For time and money to be invested in technology, there must be processes that encourage new ideas and then turn the most promising ones into full-fledged products available to customers.

In the Information Age, the driver of wealth creation is no longer financial capital but Intellectual Capital, which as described by Thomas Stewart in *Intellectual Capital* (1997) is "the sum of everything that everyone in a company knows that gives it a competitive edge.... Intellectual Capital is intellectual material—knowledge, information, intellectual property, experience—that can be put to use to create wealth."

Jack Welch, retired CEO of GE, underscored this view of Human Capital in the 1990s when he said, "We are trying to differentiate GE competitively by raising as much intellectual and creative capital from our workforce as we possibly can. That is a lot tougher than raising financial capital, which a strong company can find in any market in the world."

Employees become primary sources of a company's Intellectual

Capital and thus valuable assets. To get and keep the best minds and to facilitate innovation and creativity, leaders focus on creating a culture of learning and intellectual exploration: a learning organization. Peter Senge declared in *The Fifth Discipline* (1990) that "The organizations that will truly excel in the future will be the organizations that discover how to tap people's commitment and capacity to learn at *all* levels in an organization."

To succeed individually and as a company, the mantra is to "Work smarter." Many managers, however, still concentrate on exhorting people (merely) to work harder, a vestige of the Industrial Age.

A profound shift in funding of business takes place as we move from the Industrial to the Information Age. Companies that have amassed considerable Intellectual Capital can "buy" the financial capital they need to get up and running and to commercialize their technology. This is the reverse of the Industrial Age, where financial capital funds the firm in the process buying whatever assets—and expertise—are needed to succeed. Even those engaged in finding companies that want to raise more financial capital comment that they must bring more than money to the table. Money is now just a commodity. They have to bring more, such as expertise in the industry that the company they want to invest in can use.

Relationship Age

In the Relationship Age, companies recognize the power of human relationships, not merely to get customers or to create collaborative relationships, but as a business model. Avon Products, for example, a direct marketing company, shows that business can be done through person-to-person relationships just as easily and even more profitably than through mass marketing and advertising. Indeed, the success of these companies is built as much, if not more, on the strength of their relationships with customers and their own employees as it is on the features, quality, or prices of its products.

Companies create and maintain a vibrant network of suppliers, distributors, sales representatives, customers, strategic partners, employees—whatever drives the business. They manage the flow of human energy and spirit to make meetings go more collaboratively, to satisfy customers, to take prudent risks, to pull together to get it done.

Management recognizes and invites the full array of human energy to work, not just the energies of the body and mind, but also the energies of the human spirit. In other words, Relationship Age companies add Spiritual Capital to the financial and intellectual capital needed to gain competitive advantage.

Spiritual Capital is the additional aspect of Human Capital that becomes important in a Relationship Age company. It provides the fuel that powers the relationships through which the human energies of the company flow.

While Intellectual Capital springs from the Minds of people, Spiritual Capital springs from Human Spirit—from the Emotions, Heart, and Will. Spiritual Capital is the energy of Human Spirit which, when fully expressed in service to the highest good for all those connected with and affected by the company, fuels corporate success in its broadest sense. This means employee fulfillment, the serving of customers, respect for the community and the environment at large, as well as sustainable financial success.

Spiritual Capital manifests in companies in the form of high purpose, ethical values, collaboration, a caring and respectful attitude toward customers (and fellow employees), and respect for the community and the environment at large. Spiritual Capital is measured by surveys of employee morale and customer satisfaction.

Herb Kelleher, founder and former CEO of Southwest Airlines, described this form of Human Capital in explaining how he created competitive advantage for his airline:

> *"I've tried to create a culture of caring for people in the totality of their lives, not just at work. … The intangibles are more important than the tangibles. Someone can go out and buy airplanes from Boeing and put up ticket counters, but they can't buy our culture, our esprit de corps."*

Some time ago, I designed and facilitated an off-site strategic planning conference for the senior management of a major publishing company. I began the conference by sharing what executives had told me regarding how they felt about the direction of the company during our one-on-one discussions. This start helped shift the energy of the organization. These executives had never met together to discuss weighty issues like this and were hesitant about the conference, but hearing a montage of what their colleagues had said opened the doors and facilitated the flow of information, perspectives, and energy. By the end of the conference, the executives had opened their own lines of communication—and had begun to form their own flow of energy.

A client who founded and leads a high tech company providing data management software to financial institutions and companies in other industries that utilize massive amounts of data in their day-to-day operations commented that he sees his role as energizing the company. The funding comes largely from outside sources. The technology also comes from others. He is not a technologist. He is an energizer and organizer.

The Evolution of Human Motivation

With the human dimension as central to the Relationship Age, motivation becomes an important force shaping businesses.

Abraham Maslow gave the business community a wonderful tool for understanding motivation.

Thanks in large part to the freedom that our society's economic progress has given us, we are no longer destined to be immersed only in a struggle for (physical) survival. The lower levels of needs are being satisfied for a larger percentage of the population. As a result, we have the opportunity to rise up Maslow's Hierarchy of Needs pyramid to pursue the fulfillment of higher needs.

A powerful adaptation of Maslow's work comes from Chip Conley, owner of Joie de Vivre, a hospitality company. In his 2007 book, *PEAK: How Great Companies Get Their Mojo From Maslow,* he organizes Maslow's pyramid around three levels.

A leading pharmaceutical company asked me to design and lead strategic thinking conferences for groups of its field sales and marketing managers from around the world. In one segment, I described the concept of "competitive advantage" and engaged participants in a discussion of what the sources of such competitive advantage might be for their chief competitor—and for their own company. As expected, their initial answers focused on research and a pipeline of great pharmaceutical products. After observing how this group of diverse professionals from all over the world worked so well together, I asked them to consider yet another source of competitive advantage—one not readily seen by observers (the best kind). I shared that during the few days I worked with them, I had observed a sense of mutual respect which had engendered listening and collaboration—unusual in the corporate world—yet a quality that can turn an organization of average players into winners when it comes to creating competitive advantage. Organizational culture thus becomes a source of competitive advantage.

Relationship Truth: The Employee Pyramid

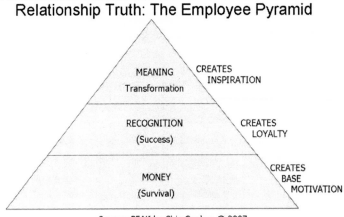

Source: PEAK by Chip Conley, @ 2007

At the lowest level, Conley observes, people are striving to meet physical needs. This is about money. This is what we mean by a *"Job."* At the middle level, people are pursuing success and recognition. This is a *"Career."* At the top level, people are pursuing transformation—essentially the opportunity to grow spiritually. At this level, we experience our work as a *"Calling."*

As people rise through these levels, serving others becomes increasingly part of their motivation. At the lowest level, it is all about "me"—my survival and physical well being. At the second level, it becomes more about others, as we seek recognition for our success. At the third level, it becomes more altruistic, as a part of our calling is to serve the world in some way, whether at the individual level or at a more global level.

This rising up the motivation pyramid represents a sea change from just a few generations ago, when the vast majority of people in the workforce were striving just to make money to survive. Now more and more people, having met their physical needs, experience the desire for thriving by finding and expressing a calling, in the process transforming themselves and serving others. This becomes a powerful resource for companies participating in the Relationship Age.

Human Capital in the Relationship Age

The Relationship Age calls for a new, expanded definition of Human Capital, one that includes not only Intellectual Capital, but also Spiritual Capital. While Intellectual Capital draws on the energies of the Mind, Spiritual Capital draws on the energy of Human Spirit [see page 166].

Companies energized by Human Spirit become powerful players in

HUMAN CAPITAL
An Evolving Concept

	CURRENT VIEW **Information Age**	EMERGING VIEW **Relationship Age**
Human Capital made up of ...	Human Capital is essentially INTELLECTUAL CAPITAL	Human Capital also includes SPIRITUAL CAPITAL
Its Nature & Economic Role:	"is the sum of everything everybody in a company knows that gives it a competitive edge....." (Stewart, 1997[1])	"is the energy of human spirit flowing through the company's relationships that fuels its success" (Gillett, 2000 [2])
Human Capital draws on the Energies of	The Human MIND	The Human SPIRIT
Its Importance	Replaced Financial & Physical Capital as Driver of Wealth Creation[3]	Provides a new source of Competitive Advantage and Wealth Creation
Especially for	Information & Technology-based Industries	Relationship-based Industries
RELATED CONCEPTS & STRATEGIES		
Key People in the Org	"Knowledge Workers"[4] (Drucker, 1959)	"Light Workers"[5] Bringing their Spirit to Work
Hire for	Knowledge & Experience	Attitude & Energy
The Organization	The "Learning Organization"[6] (Senge, 1990)	A Network of Relationships through which human energy flows
The Leader...	Extracts, organizes & applies knowledge	Inspires and energizes people to achieve the firm's highest purpose
How CEOs in each realm see the path to success	"We are trying to differentiate GE competitively by raising as much intellectual and creative capital from our workforce as we possibly can. That is a lot tougher than raising financial capital, which a strong company can find in any market in the world." —Jack Welch, CEO, GE (1990s)	"I've tried to create a culture of caring for people in the totality of their lives, not just at work.... The intangibles are more important than the tangibles. Someone can go out and buy airplanes from Boeing and ticket counters, but they can't buy our culture, our esprit de corps." —Herb Kelleher, retired CEO, Southwest Airlines

1. *Intellectual Capital* by Thomas Stewart (1997)
2. As described in Gillett's 2000 booklet *Spiritual Capital: Building Vibrant Businesses That Serve Shareholders and Humanity*
3. *Free to Choose* by Milton Friedman (1981)
4. "One who works primarily with information or one who develops and uses knowledge in the workplace."—Wikipedia
5. See Chapter 13
6. *The Fifth Discipline* by Peter Senge (1990)

business. Organizational processes are less about efficiency and output and more about the energy of creativity, innovation, inspiration, and collaboration. These companies focus on relationships and the energy that flows through them.

Southwest Airlines puts this into practice with their hiring philosophy: "We hire for attitude, not necessarily for aptitude—with the exception of pilots," said Kevin Krone, Southwest's vice president of marketing, sales, and distribution. "Investing the time to find the person with the right attitude is critical." Indeed, under the leadership of maverick CEO Herb Kelleher, Southwest Airlines broke all the rules and created new ones. Fun was not only allowed but became rampant. The company focused not just on its role—to fly a traveler from one place to another—but also on the total experience travelers and employees have.

Companies like Southwest Airlines attract and motivate people who build the spiritual capital of the company. Just as the people who help build their companies' Intellectual Capital with their brain power and experience are called "knowledge workers," those who bring their whole selves to work, including their Human Spirit, can be called "light workers." Light workers help focus energies on the highest purposes of the company and help build and energize the human relationships that make the company successful.

Summary

Even though our economy has largely moved beyond the Industrial Age, unfortunately many managers and companies retain, almost hard-wired, the beliefs about what's needed in people, the human organization, and management practices that evolved in the Industrial Age. Managers seek to make their mark by demanding efficiency—and zero defects—not only in the output of the company but in the functioning of the human organization. The organization is viewed as a machine, and employees succeed by "Working Harder."

In the Information Age, this has shifted so that creativity, innovation, and continual learning and improvement replace the Industrial Age focus on material resources and human labor. The Information Age is powered by Human Capital, specifically in the form of Intellectual Capital. The organization is a learning organization, and people succeed by "Working Smarter."

In the Relationship Age, with an additional form of Human Capital— namely Spiritual Capital—companies call on people to bring all of themselves to work, not just Mind and Body, but also Human Spirit, including Emotions, Heart, and Will.

The organization of the Relationship Age is a vibrant network of human relationships (with employees, but also customers, vendors and community). The mantra of people in the Relationship Age is to "Work with Purpose and Passion."

Whatever industry you are in, you can utilize the principles of all these ages, recognizing that the management principles needed now are far different from the Industrial Age. Plus, a new model of business is needed to reflect the advent of the Relationship Age, the subject of the next chapter.

CHAPTER 13

THE NOBLE BUSINESS ENTERPRISE

Noble: possessing, characterized by, or arising from superiority of mind or character or of ideals or morals.

—Merriam-Webster Online dictionary

As I talked with those involved in the Unitel/AT&T Canada LDS turnaround and reflected on their stories, I began to see that there was an underlying quality that helped power their uncommon achievement: nobility. In leaders and employees alike, nobility pervaded their thinking, their relationships, their sense of purpose, their actions, and their very character.

I first saw and felt that nobility in CEO Bill Catucci's office as he shared the turnaround story with excitement and joy. I then saw that same nobility in the lobby of the Toronto office building where the people of AT&T Canada LDS gathered to honor their leader and to celebrate what they had achieved and experienced together. In his parting words to his colleagues, Bill pointed to this nobility when he said:

> *"You've got a lot to be proud of. This company is one of the leading compa-*
> *nies in Canada. Who would have thought that possible just three years ago?*
> *One of the main reasons we are is because of the kind of people standing*
> *right here. I see people of integrity, people of good will, people who respect*
> *others, and people who truly care about customers. Keep vigilance about our*
> *values. Keep nurturing that spirit that we created together."*

Imagine a company powered by nobility. What would it look like and how would it succeed? First, Noble Enterprises have the following characteristics:

1. They see themselves as serving the world—not in the sense of providing products or services to every person or organization, but

169

rather in the sense of viewing their purpose as making the world a better place through the impact of their services and products and the impact of how they operate. Thus they see their role in serving the common good.

2. They see their purpose as not just serving financial shareholders, but serving all of their constituencies. In doing this, they believe they will be a more successful company, one that achieves long-term, sustainable success.

3. They honor their employees, their customers, and their communities by *how* they view and interact with these groups.

4. They marshal not only the energies of Body and Mind, but also of Human Spirit, in the process fostering self-actualization of employees, sterling service to customers, and expanded performance even with vendors.

5. They accomplish great business results—not in spite of being noble, but rather because of this very nobility. These are long-term results, not spikes in quarterly financial performance.

This Noble Business Enterprise model puts the human being at the center. Furthermore, it recognizes the role and power of the Human Spirit ingredient, as well as the role of human mind.

How do Noble Business Enterprises achieve superior business performance?

1. By recognizing the inner dimension (people's motivation, character, and spirit) and building it into its modus operandi—from hiring practices to leadership practices to reward and promotion processes.

2. By seeing and responding not only to the material needs of customers and employees, but also to their inner spiritual and

emotional needs and aspirations.

3. By building relationships with their employees, customers, vendors, and communities characterized by the highest ethics and sense of higher purpose, through which great energy flows to serve that purpose.

4. By drawing from the best of business principles and building nobility into those practices to make them even more effective.

Noble Business Enterprises don't just happen. They are created and led by Noble Leaders throughout the company who bring their high character to work for the good of the company in serving its high goals. More on this in the next chapter.

Building a Noble Business Enterprise From the Ground Up

How does one build a Noble Business Enterprise from scratch?

When N.R. Narayan Murthy and six colleagues set out in 1981 to build a global company, they wanted to capitalize on the trend toward globalization.† They had scraped together starting capital of $250. Though they recognized the challenges of starting a business in socialist India with its bureaucratic hurdles (it took them two years to acquire a computer), they were determined to succeed.

Twenty-five years later, at the time of Murthy's retirement, Infosys Technologies Ltd, had become India's leading IT company. Their customer base had expanded to hundreds from one, employees had grown to 58,000 from seven, and market capitalization had risen to $20 *billion* from only $250.

Reflecting back on the challenge of how to build such a company, Murthy said:

"First, think about what sort of company you want to have. Corporations must reach out to society and build goodwill if they aspire to longevity. This is especially true in India, where our success contrasts with widespread poverty. We always ask ourselves: Are we adding value for our

---

†This story is taken largely from a piece written by Narayan Murthy in a September 29, 2006, *Wall Street Journal* article entitled "Clear Conscience—Clear Profit."

clients and society? Are we following Gandhi's dictum, to 'be the change in the world you want to see'? This does not translate into outright charity, which saps recipients' self-esteem, but to empowering people. For example, we train and employ poor mothers in the villages surrounding our Bangalore campus, giving them a stake in society."

Revitalizing Stagnant Companies by Transforming Them into Noble Business Enterprises

The Noble Business Enterprise model is not only for those who are just starting out to build a company. It is equally applicable to existing companies. It can help failing or stagnant companies become successful. The Unitel/AT&T Canada LDS example in Part II is one such example. Catucci's next turnaround, Equifax, though not failing, was stagnant and needed a transfusion.

Five Pillars of the Noble Enterprise

What sets Noble Business Enterprises apart from others is human energy and how that energy is generated and used.

Noble Business Enterprises create an organizational and management culture of nobility with five "pillars" of nobility.

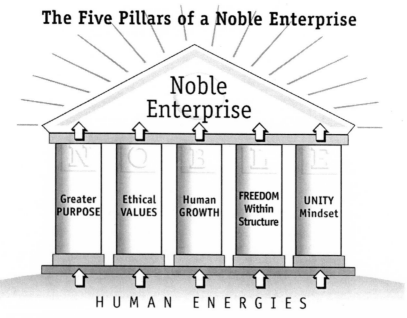

The Five Pillars of a Noble Enterprise

Noble Enterprise

Greater PURPOSE | Ethical VALUES | Human GROWTH | FREEDOM Within Structure | UNITY Mindset

HUMAN ENERGIES

Each one of the pillars can provide a powerful boost to a company. When all five are active, uncommon results may become the norm. When any one of these pillars is weak or nonexistent, the entire company suffers, constricting the flow of human energy and limiting the company's business performance.

Pillar One: Greater Purpose

"To have a great purpose to work for, a purpose larger than ourselves, is one of the secrets of making life significant, for then the meaning and worth of the individual overflow his personal borders and survive his death."

—Will Durant

Greater purpose means a corporate purpose that is more than just generating profit. It is that, but it is also about serving all constituencies of the company, not just financial shareholders. This is the multiple stakeholder philosophy. But is more than that. Greater purpose also means beyond just the material dimension, serving nonmaterial needs as well as material needs.

Noble Business Enterprises with such a greater purpose attract and inspire people who are motivated not only by money by also by higher personal goals of self-actualization. Such companies then align people around a greater purpose.

Companies with a greater purpose are well-positioned to thrive, generating both great employee morale and superior business performance. Recall that before Bill Catucci took over at Unitel, the company's focus was primarily on cutting costs in an attempt to stem the cash drain. As CEO, Catucci focused the company on achieving a powerful mission, which generated excitement and commitment, leading eventually to a rapid turnaround.

When people pursue a greater purpose, they tend to reach down for more, to go the extra mile. And they grow and achieve more. A greater purpose focuses employees on common enterprise in a company, enabling them to see the whole picture so that they can contribute to it.

Greater purpose is about service—serving others and humanity, serving the planet, serving the deepest yearnings and spiritual goals of people who are involved with the company in any role.

When Kazuma Tateisi founded the Omron Corporation (Japan) in 1933, he chose as his corporate motto: ***"At work for a better life, a*** *better world for all"* (emphasis added). It was his way of sharing his belief that a company should work for the benefit of society.

From his perspective, the real purpose of a company was to serve society, and only when that was achieved, should the company earn any profits and growth.

Today, still espousing their founder's philosophy, Tokyo-based Omron uses its sensing and control technology to promote business operations essential for the convenience and comfort of society by seeking to accurately extract important information from various phenomena and turn it into new value. They provide products and services for a range of markets, including industrial automation, electronic components, automotive electronics, social systems, and healthcare. By 2005, net sales had reached nearly 627 billion yen and net income nearly 35.8 billion yen.

Greater purpose is also about serving employees. David Neeleman, founder of three successive profitable airlines, most recently CEO of JetBlue Airways, described in a recent talk how he focused on serving employees. In response to a question about how he explains (and justifies) to Wall Street (whose main concern is the "serving" of shareholders) this emphasis on serving the *employee*, Neeleman responded, "We serve our *employees*, who serve our *customers*, who serve our *shareholders.*"

In serving others, building a trusting and caring relationship with people is the foundation, not merely going after sales transactions to fill a specific need. The relationship is the proverbial "golden goose" from which sales transactions emanate—as well as collaborations to create new products and greater value.

Mary Lou Andre founded Organization by Design, Inc., her Needham, Massachusetts, company, to help individuals improve and manage their wardrobes for success. As the company began to grow, her role expanded beyond wardrobe advisor: In addition to providing clients with the services they requested, she also provided the personal support and guidance they needed to discard limiting beliefs, develop positive thinking, and build confidence. In sharing her own sense of purpose with fellow business owners in a peer advisory leadership group that I helped lead, she explained that she saw her greater purpose as that of uplifting people and increasing their inner confidence as well as (and through) improving their outer physical appearance.

A greater purpose means being mindful of all the constituencies that your business enterprise affects, both in terms of the resources it draws on and the impact it has. Rather than ask "What trade-offs do we need to make between competing constituencies?" the Noble Enterprise asks "How can we operate in a way that serves all?"

Pillar Two. Ethical Values

"I've tried to create a culture of caring for people in the totality of their lives, not just at work. There's no magic formula. It's like building a giant mosaic—It takes thousands of little pieces."

—Herb Kelleher, former CEO, Southwest Airlines

The trend to build values into companies is an important step toward a Noble Business Enterprise. These values are not merely a perk to make a company a more pleasant place to work. They become one of the ways that a Noble Business Enterprise builds success. Hence, they constitute the second pillar of a Noble Business Enterprise.

In Noble Enterprises, such values are neither vague platitudes nor empty promises. They are calls to action.

When N.R. Narayan Murthy (who, as we saw earlier in this chapter, helped build a $20 billion IT company in India) reflected back twenty-five years to when he and his partners founded Infosys Technologies Ltd., he pointed to the importance of values in addressing the considerable challenges of building a successful global company:†

"While we recognized the challenges (of building a global IT company), we were certain of our value system. We believed that great companies are built to last hundreds of years, which requires a foundation that goes beyond revenues, profits and market capitalization. We pledged to seek respect from our stakeholders, which would automatically lead us to do the right thing by each of them. We would satisfy customers, be fair to employees, follow the highest principles in dealing with investors, and make

† N.R. Narayan Murthy. "Clear Conscience—Clear Profit." *Wall Street Journal* (September 29, 2006)

a positive difference to society. If we did that, we agreed, revenue and profit would follow."

When Bill Catucci set out to create the values for struggling Unitel, he turned to the employees and asked them to come up with the company's values. The risk, he thought, was that they might come up with values that were not high values, such as merely "we want to make a lot of money." He was pleasantly surprised when the values they came back with were good strong values. (see Chapter 5).

Values by themselves are not necessarily powerful drivers of high performance. But when they are ethical values—values that reflect a respect for and connection with other people (and all of life)—they generate more enthusiasm, commitment, and action, as we saw in the AT&T Canada LDS example.

Every company and every CEO determines what ethical values are most important to them. Involving employees in the process of selecting the company's values, and exploring what they mean in practice, as we saw with the AT&T Canada LDS story, can help embed those values into the minds and hearts of all employees.

Here are some ethical values that Noble Business Enterprises espouse and live:

> *Integrity and Honesty.* In the case of AT&T Canada LDS, one of the important noble values they came up with was Integrity and Honesty. This was important to them because the company had been portrayed in the business press as unethical before Bill arrived.

> *Truth.* Truth is a powerful value. When we speak the truth about a situation, we can proceed to deal with it. Conversely, when we invent lies about what is, then we waste energy and delay appropriate action.

> *Respect.* When we have respect for coworkers, customers, and employees, we will elicit their best.

> *Courage.* Caving in to pressure or delaying decisions until we "have all the necessary information" is the easy way out. It takes courage to

make a decision when others would avoid it, or to take unpopular (yet necessary) actions.

Reliability. Doing what we say we will helps build better relationships of trust.

Trust. When we trust others, they usually prove us right. When we distrust them, they also prove us right by fulfilling our (low) expectations.

Caring. When people feel that others truly care, they are more willing to listen, to contribute, to trust—all the good values above. Thus, caring about others is also an important value, not only in customer service, but in management.

A participant in the peer advisory leadership group mentioned earlier, Ken Boroson of Boroson Architects in New Haven, Connecticut, shared with the group early on, "My leadership page is blank." He chose to put values first in leading his firm, even when presenting to a potential client. Rather than first showing pictures of his firm's work, he led off his presentations by describing his firm's values. Later, reflecting on the power of values-based leadership (and the support of his colleagues in the peer advisory group), he commented, "This group has solidified my moving in a new leadership direction both personally and business-wise...I have to believe that our recent growth—350 percent over the prior year, with an increase of only 140 percent in people costs—is a direct result of what's come out of this group."

Pillar Three. Human Growth

"We know what we are, but know not what we may be."

—William Shakespeare

Most companies want growth—that is, business growth in revenues and profits. Noble Business Enterprises also work at growing the *people* that make up the company. Thus, just as some companies build cultures of continuous improvement, Noble Business Enterprises build cultures of continuous human growth.

A company's commitment to human as well as business growth attracts good employees, people who want continually to learn and expand their capabilities. This commitment also helps to keep them.

When most companies set out to provide growth opportunities for employees, they usually focus on learning new skills so the employees can perform better or step up to a higher level of responsibility. With their emphasis on the whole human being, Noble Business Enterprises provide opportunities to grow not just the mind, but also the whole person.

Thus, in Noble Enterprises, human growth is about professional and personal growth. Noble Enterprises provide employees not only with opportunities to learn new skills, but also with opportunities to develop personal growth, such as leadership and relationships skills, and to build character. A company's Intellectual and Spiritual Capital increase as a result.

For example, Catucci and his team created the AT&T Canada University, before the company had even become profitable. Employees could learn new skills relevant to their jobs. They could also learn leadership skills. And there were opportunities to explore their own sense of purpose, their calling in life. This process not only helped employees choose new career paths, but also helped them see how their work contributed to their own personal and professional growth.

The payoff was not just at some point in the future, when employees would have learned new skills, but right away in terms of greater employee commitment to the company and enthusiasm for their work and for achieving the company's mission. AT&T Canada's low employee turnover rate was in part a reflection of employees' positive feelings about the opportunities they had for personal and professional growth.

Pillar Four. Freedom Within Structure

"Groups become great only when everyone in them, leaders and members alike, is free to do his or her absolute best."

—Warren Bennis and Patricia Ward Biederman

All companies want empowered people—employees and managers who take initiative, who get things done, who are entrepreneurial, in short, employees who are energized. But how does a company do this? Is it through motivational speakers, communication from the top, incentives and rewards?

One of the best ways to get empowered people is simply to *allow* them to be empowered. To take away the constraints that keep them from feeling empowered. The idea of freedom as a powerful force for human and business progress is, of course, not new.

In fact, the revolutionary idea of freedom burst forth nearly simultaneously in 1776 on two separate continents. The American colonies, in their Declaration of Independence, not only claimed independence but also made audacious claims about equality, rights, and governments instituted to serve the people.

> *We hold these truths to be self-evident, that all men are created equal, that they are endowed by their Creator with certain unalienable Rights, that among these are Life, Liberty and the pursuit of Happiness. — That to secure these rights, Governments are instituted among Men, deriving their just powers from the consent of the governed.*
> — U.S. Declaration of Independence

Meanwhile in Scotland, Adam Smith claimed in the *Wealth of Nations* that an entire nation does better economically when in the marketplace each person is free to maximize his or her own economic benefit without regard to the whole.

> *Every individual….generally, indeed, neither intends to promote the public interest, nor knows how much he is promoting it. By preferring the support of domestic to that of foreign industry he intends only his own security; and by directing that industry in such a manner as its produce may be of the greatest value, he intends only his own gain, and he is in this, as in many other cases, led by an invisible hand to promote an end which was no part of his intention.*
> —Adam Smith, *The Wealth of Nations*, Book IV, Chapter II

History has borne out the power of freedom. Countries that are free—both politically and economically—tend to have the highest standards of living and the highest economic growth rates.

Ironically, there has not been the same recognition of or reverence for freedom *within* most companies. For most large and many small companies, individual freedom is not a core value and is often viewed as a threat to management power and operating efficiency.

Interestingly, when I present the Noble Enterprise model to graduate business school classes, invariably, it is this pillar, that of freedom, that they feel most needs strengthening in their company—both for their own development and contribution and for the company's benefit.

Bearing out this observation is the story of William Gore and the creation of W.L. Gore & Associates, Inc, eventually makers of Gore-Tex. Before founding the company, Gore found in his job at DuPont that when he was involved on a project team that there was more creativity and fulfillment compared to working within the traditional hierarchical structure. As W.L. Gore & Associates grew, he built a management structure and management process to incorporate the best of the project management system, including trust and freedom.†

People often resent and feel stifled by structure. In yearning to be free of such constraints, they think they want *no* structure, but most people need a logical underpinning for their job and for the whole company. Such freedom, balanced with responsibility for one's own actions and for cocreating the company's success, creates a powerful channel for the flow of human energy.

Noble Business Enterprises trust that benefits will result from giving employees the freedom to explore, to experiment, and to take prudent risks. Such companies have a management system that not only allows and encourages this freedom but also provides an overall framework within which people can work on their own to further the company's interests. As Bill Catucci put it:

> *"If you tell me what we're trying to accomplish and why, and then leave me alone, I may actually be able to come up with a better way to get there than if you tell me exactly what to do.*
>
> *"I can't watch three thousand people. I'm going to give them the foundation—the vision, the values, the strategy and management system, and then hope that we're aligned. Then they're independent; they're on their own. They're going to do their thing, and you know what? They may actually achieve more than what you had expected. And because they've done it on their own, they feel better about themselves. That is the model.*

---

†See www.fundinguniverse.com/company-histories/WL-Gore-amp;-Associates-Inc-Company-History.html. See also an *Inc* magazine cover story article of August 1982 titled "The Un-Manager."

Provide the foundation and get them the tools to work with, so they can do what they want. In that way, they better themselves professionally and personally and innovate, and by doing so, they improve the company."

Noble Enterprises trust the motivation and collective wisdom of their employees, just as two generations ago Douglas McGregor, in his 1960 book *The Human Side of Enterprise*, envisioned a workforce made up of Theory Y workers, people who are motivated by the desire for self-actualization (as opposed to Theory X workers, who work only because they "have to" to make a living). For example, Yvon Chouinaar, a passionate climber and surfer, founded Patagonia, a successful company of over a thousand people, after creating superior equipment for mountain climbers. In his book, *Let My People Go Surfing: The Education of a Reluctant Businessman*, he offers his management philosophy: "Just give them general direction; then leave them alone!" He also throws out the idea of conventional work hours. Employees can take off whenever they want; they just need to get the work done.

Managers in Noble Business Enterprises let go of the notion of control as the ultimate management tool and replace it, as we saw in the AT&T Canada LDS example, with an overall context consisting of the mission, values, and strategy of the company, a management system that facilitates prudent risk-taking, and an inspiring leadership that encourages people to take initiative. The pace of progress there surprised everyone inside and outside the company. One of the lessons is that people who are free to pursue and implement the best solutions can achieve remarkable results.

Pillar Five. Unity Mindset

"Everything is connected… no one thing can change by itself."
—Paul Hawken

When people see the interconnections among all of the elements that make up their environment, they have a Unity Mindset. In a Noble Business Enterprise, customers, employees, union members, executives, suppliers, the outside community, the physical environment, and more are not just separate entities but are all powerfully connected through a web of relationships.

The Unity Mindset is more than just a way of *understanding* the world as totally interconnected. It is also a way of *interacting* with that world in a frame of mind (and heart) that says, "We are one." Albert Einstein put it this way:

> *"We are part of the whole which we call the universe, but it is an optical delusion of our mind that we think we are separate. This separateness is like a prison for us. Our job is to widen the circle of our compassion so we feel connected with all people and situations."*

When people work in such a "real world," they are more effective. For example, recall that when Bill Catucci became CEO of struggling Unitel, he faced a demoralized workforce, particularly among the union ranks. They were angry at the company for decisions that outsourced work. There was a huge gulf between the union and management.

To breach this gulf, he needed to see and treat the union members as part of the "us" of the company, rather than as the "enemy." Rather than focus on the economics of outsourcing versus not outsourcing, he focused on the Human Economics of Spirit and Unity. It was this latter reality that he chose to see and act from—and it made all the difference, for it awakened that reality with union members also. This and other acts of unity thinking and collaboration led to a dramatic turnaround in relations with the union, which turned from antagonistic to collaborative.

Catucci's success stemmed not so much from great negotiating techniques but rather from an underlying view that *we're all in this together, and we won't succeed without all of us in the same boat, rowing together.* Out of a sense of common ground with the union, he created unity with mutual respect, shared purpose, and thus collaboration. In essence, he created a unified energy field of human endeavor.

Noble Business Enterprises view this spirit of collaboration, rather than of competition, as the true source of success, because they recognize that it is the desire to excel and willingness to collaborate that leads to superior performance.†
Project teams, self-directed work teams, and executive teams unleash creativity, innovation, enthusiasm, and risk-taking. Strategic alliances are examples of this kind of shared purpose and collaboration that cross corporate boundaries.

When members of a company see and act from a belief in a totally interconnected world, it is a natural step to serve the stakeholders that the company affects in other ways. Recall that AT&T Canada LDS became active

---

†Alfie Kohn makes a compelling argument in his 1986, 1992 book *No Competition: The Case Against Competition* that competition is not really the effective force people think it is. Based on his research, Kohn concludes that in field after field, it isn't the desire to beat someone else that generates superior performance, but rather the desire to excel, to accomplish. Furthermore, he contends that it is not competition but rather the ability to work cooperatively together that enables us to succeed. See also "How to Succeed Without Even Vying" by Kohn in the September 1986 *Psychology Today*.

in the United Way, outperforming far larger companies, and provided assistance during emergencies. This made people proud to work for AT&T Canada and elevated their image in the community, but, more, it was just a natural thing to reach out and serve their community.

A client, Steve Hall, founded and leads Chandler LLC, a Connecticut firm that provides planning and management services for building projects. This involves dealing with the complex world of architectural design, building engineering, and construction methods. It also involves managing the relationships between architects, other design and engineering professionals, contractors, and owners so that projects run smoothly and are cost effective.

In the course of overseeing projects totaling more than $1.5 billion in value, Steve observed that lack of talent, resources, or information are rarely responsible for a project falling short of expectations. Instead, projects suffer because of poor working relationships. Problems can usually be traced to situations where key participants on the team do not share similar values, agendas and objectives or where communication is closed.

To avoid such situations, Steve and the building project owner assemble a team of independent project members who share a set of seven values that Steve has found to be the foundation of a successful project:

1. Mutual respect
2. Honesty
3. Responsibility
4. Accountability
5. Trust that all will do their best
6. Common welfare of all in creating successful project
7. Success for the owner is success for all

Steve, in essence, functions as the "CEO" of this temporary team assembled to plan and execute the project. Unity of purpose is the driver for success, so when project participants share a Unity Mindset of purpose and values, the likelihood of a "win/win" result is greatly increased.

Steve observes, "Creating unity is hard work and not always successful. Some owners and participants only give it lip service and maintain their desire to drive the project with short-term, least-cost parameters. This is rarely successful in creating the desired long-term results."

By extending his Unity Mindset toward higher value and purpose, Steve has become a champion of green building design. He promotes green building both because it is good for the environment and because it makes good financial sense for the owner. For example, he helped the Princeton Club of New York City utilize self-generation of power as the cornerstone of a renewal project to position the club for the twenty-first century. At its core, Steve observes, the Unity Mindset involves "moving beyond just conservation and mitigation of damage to an attitude of 'regenesis' where all that we do or make or build must create positive results and energy for ourselves and for the world."†

At the Center of the Noble Enterprise

"The most powerful weapon on earth is the human soul on fire."

—Field Marshall Ferdinand Foch

Knowledge workers have been at the core of twentieth century knowledge-based businesses in what we described earlier as the Information Age. Noble Enterprises have at their core light workers. Light workers hold the vision of the greater purpose for a company. They live and encourage the ethical values of how the company operates. They help build the relationships through which people's energies flow to do the company's "business."

In short, light workers bring their "souls on fire" to work. One vivid example happened at the 150-year-old Malden Mills Company in Lawrence, Massachusetts. On a December evening in 1995, fire destroyed all but one of its four buildings. Even before the fire, this last remaining textile company in New England was in danger of going under due to global competitive forces.

Watching the fire devour his company's buildings that evening, however, Aaron Feuerstein, Malden's owner and CEO, vowed that the fire would not put his company out of business. His subsequent actions have become legend in corporate social responsibility circles. The very next day, he announced that he would rebuild the company. And, rather than lay off employees, he continued to pay them even as the buildings were being rebuilt and replacement equipment being installed.††

Less known were the actions of fourteen employees who also watched the fire engulf Malden's buildings that night. In their own way, what they subsequently did that night played as important a role in saving Malden Mills as their CEO, for these fourteen brave souls took it on themselves to go into

---

†See www.regenesisgroup.com for more information.
††See "Malden Mills: A Study in Leadership" at www.opi-inc.com/malden.htm

one of the buildings and stay throughout the long night to protect it from the fire. By morning, their actions had succeeded in largely saving that one building and the important pieces of equipment and materials in it.

Feuerstein credits them with keeping the doors open. Their actions enabled the company to continue serving some of their key customers.

While Feuerstein's actions had given the company a longer term future, the fourteen employees' actions had enabled the company to keep shipping product to its customers, even while they rebuilt, thereby also enhancing their chances of long term success.

While knowledge workers provide the Intellectual Capital of the firm, light workers, like those described above, provide its Spiritual Capital. Bill Catucci called forth this kind of spirit at AT&T Canada and in his subsequent role at Equifax.

Light workers bring strong, positive emotional and spiritual energies to the organization. They are interested in, care about, and develop good rapport with other people. They enjoy working together. They have an indomitable will to succeed, because they willingly take responsibility and have a "Get it done!" mentality. Light workers have an innate ability to connect with others and a desire to serve others. They assume a sense of "we" rather than "me" in situations where others may be divisive and fractious. They build powerful relationships with others within and outside the company. By their willingness to surmount business challenges, they help to achieve large corporate goals. They want to make a difference in the world, to serve a higher purpose than self.

While knowledge workers bring great knowledge to work and help create and utilize the company's Intellectual Capital, light workers bring great Human Spirit to work and help create and utilize the company's Spiritual Capital.

While knowledge workers help create a Return on Intelligence and Intellectual Property, light workers help create a Return on Spirit and Integrity.

Light workers draw on Heart energy, as well as Emotional energy and Will energy, to help organizations develop a sense of interconnection, to generate enthusiasm, and to create the discipline needed to achieve great progress.

People who become part of a Noble Business Enterprise begin to think, feel, and act in concert with Human Spirit, freedom, and interconnectedness. As they do, they bring these qualities into the rest of their lives. When they leave their company, they take them wherever they go, thereby enriching the enterprises they join or lead and the communities in which they operate.

CHAPTER 14

THE NOBLE LEADER

"The golden core of leadership is the ability to raise aspirations. Aspiration doesn't just build companies, it builds civilizations. It changes a set of ordinary people into a team of extraordinary talents, empowering them to convert plausible impossibilities into convincing possibilities."
—N.R. Narayana Murthy, cofounder, nonexecutive chairman, and chief mentor of Infosys Technologies Ltd (India)

"Leadership is a potent combination of strategy and character. But if you must be without one, be without the strategy."
—Norman Schwarzkopf

Educational degrees, work experience, and sharp decision-making and organizing skills are important in bringing about the kind of performance gains illustrated by the story of Unitel/AT&T. Ultimately, however, qualities of character and spirit equip leaders to achieve such results. Leaders with strong inner qualities achieve the big leaps in corporate performance. They are Noble Leaders.

Years ago on a flight from the U.S. to Japan, one of my colleagues noticed shortly after takeoff that the man sitting next to him was hunched over in his seat with his hands tightly clasped. Thinking that the man was afraid of flying, he tried to calm him by making some idle conversation, then added, "Don't worry. We're safer here than we were in the taxi getting to the airport."

The man turned his head and said, "Oh, no, I'm not afraid. I was just meditating and praying." Embarrassed at having misjudged the situation and interrupted the man, my colleague apologized and turned away. The man said, "No, no. I must explain. I have just been made executive vice president of Mitsui. I was praying that I would be worthy of the people reporting to me."

Noble Leaders understand that *who* they are plays as important a role in achieving success as what they *do*. Noble Leaders also see their role as more comprehensive and far reaching than do traditional leaders.

The CHARACTER of the Noble Business Leader

Traditional views of leadership focus on the outer *doing* part, the action techniques that leaders use. But the inner *being* part is equally important, because people resonate with and are stirred into inspired action by a Noble Leader's inner being. This authentic self is manifested in the following ways:

A Sense of Purpose

"I didn't need this job. I was set financially. I think it's important to be compensated, but I didn't need the money. I took the job because I wanted to prove that this company could be saved—and saved by doing contrarian things, like addressing the human dimension. I wanted to do something memorable. I'm here to succeed for a lot of other people. However, I want to do it in a way that I can reconcile with my values."

—Bill Catucci, former CEO, AT&T Canada LDS

When people in the ranks know that their leader's motivation is of the highest caliber, they are far more likely to be excited about giving their best to help the company succeed. If their leader is only in it for her own personal financial gain or reputation, then all those great vision and mission statements sit there empty, and all of the energies of the people in the organization lie dormant and unused. Such a leader then says, "I tried all this soft stuff, but it doesn't work!"

Recall that in the early days of Catucci's leadership at Unitel/AT&T Canada LDS, he and his top executives had nothing to sell but their highest intentions. All they could do was to point to their vision, their mission, and their values—and plans. They had no better network or array of products and services than their competitors and also did not yet have quality back up to where it should be. But they did have the burning desire to make the company the best. This was powerful enough to cause numerous current and departed customers to give them another chance.

Full Mental Powers

When we think of the Mind, we tend to think of it as the knowledge and experience people bring to their leadership. We also think of it as the analytical and decision-making abilities that leaders exercise. Yet these are only part of the power of the Mind that Noble Leaders tap. They succeed also because of their:

Perception. How we see things affects how we interact with them, solve them, and capitalize on them. The popular phrase "turning problems into opportunities" is about more than attitude; it also is about the power of perception. Noble Leaders see not just the problems in a situation, but also the seeds of a whole new way to come at an issue or a business. They also see the whole—the interconnection of everything. This enables them to solve problems and take actions that advance the total system rather than just individual problems and sub-goals.

Beliefs. Noble Leaders also tap the power of beliefs. They hold positive beliefs, even while being realistic about circumstances. Rather than believe that their employees are inadequate and view them in terms of their faults, they perceive their hidden talents and hold fast to the belief that they will come forth. The power of their mental image actually helps that happen.

Bill Catucci did not believe in limitations for Unitel/AT&T Canada. He created and nurtured a bigger vision of what could be and kept communicating that vision with enthusiasm. He pushed the company—not with fear that it would not succeed or criticism for "failure"—but rather with a deep belief that the people could and would in fact achieve the vision.

Will Power. Noble Leaders use their Will to focus energies productively on key issues, goals, and projects. This energy manifests in a clear sense of purpose, determination to get there, commitment to the work needed to succeed, a focus on what's most important, and the discipline to keep on track.

They devote this Will to the highest good—the good of their people, their customers, their shareholders, and humanity. In so doing, they often unleash additional energy from those involved. The highest good is not just people's material needs, but also their *nonmaterial* needs, which often energizes those who seek the adventure of accomplishing something good and creating greater meaning in their lives.

When the Canadian banks and AT&T asked Bill to be the CEO of Unitel, he turned down the offer several times. He was planning to retire then. But,

after a lot of soul searching with my wife, I decided to do it, not because it was a great financial opportunity, because that's not what we were expecting or intending, but because it was an opportunity to run a company, to put my own ideas into action, and to try to show that the restructure and the business plan we put in place really made sense and that we could make it work.

"This was my first opportunity to be a CEO. There's a difference in being a CEO and being a top executive. Being a CEO is different. If you're the kind of person who wants to have the buck stop at you, then that's where you want to be. You want to be able to shape things, help make the good decisions that move things. When the debate is on and people come to an impasse, you want to cast the vote that says, 'We're going to move this way or that way.'

"It's an opportunity to shape a corporation. In the case of Unitel, you're shaping the economic development and quality of life of a country. This is not small potatoes. If you've grown up believing that you're the kind of person who can make things happen and be in things that really matter, that's where you want to be. Some people don't want to be there, and that's fine. It's not a value judgment. (But) some people feel they're equipped to be in charge and that they can make a difference, and they can do things that are good.

"Because I wasn't driven by the money, I could make honest, integral decisions. I didn't have to worry that, if I lost my job, I'd be out on the street. I had no fear as a result."

Emotional Power

Noble Leaders express positive Emotional energy as part of their leadership, which in turns draws it forth in others. Such energy manifests as a strong sense of self, pride in accomplishment, team spirit, fun and humor, enthusiasm, and spontaneity.

Bill Catucci worked at getting enthusiasm down to the grass roots. While there were many ways of doing it, it was fueled by Bill's own contagious enthusiasm and positive can-do outlook. He said, "There's no silver bullet. I got it there because I was enthusiastic myself. People could argue that I was overly enthusiastic. But if you've got a team that is down in the dumps, what kind of leader do you want for your organization? You want honesty, but you also want enthusiasm and optimism about the future. I spent a lot of time communicating that positive outlook."

Heart Power

The Noble Leader taps and expresses Heart energies, which have four manifestations:

- courage to make the tough decisions, to take the risks necessary to succeed
- passion about the company, its purpose, and the programs to achieve that purpose.
- integrity to build business strength through the company's values
- caring to inspire true customer service and full collaboration.

Noble Leaders create genuine relationships and connection with employees, customers, vendors, and the community. They connect with people in a way that makes others know that they are acknowledged and cared about. Noble Leaders also awaken and encourage a spirit of "we"—and work at creating and nurturing a spirit of community. They are fully present, both with and for others.

Vincent Petrecca spent nearly his entire career at Hubbell Inc (Orange, CT), a manufacturer of electrical and electronic wiring devices and lighting equipment, working his way up from plant engineer to executive vice president with eight divisions reporting to him. His passion for product "focus" to avoid the extra (and often hidden) costs of too large a product line was legend throughout the company. This strategy, along with a strong marketing sense and ability to work with the company's distributors, enabled him to expand operations and turn around losing ones.

His success, however, was ultimately due to his leadership. A tough manager, he demanded high performance and got it. On a visit with him to one of the plants in his organization, I was surprised not to see the fear-based, judgmental and controlling behavior one might expect from a "tough" manager. Instead I saw a genuine enthusiasm and a warm connection with employees. The air was electric with energy as he walked through the plant.

Vin put as much energy into simply relating with everyone he saw as he did in examining new equipment or a new product or addressing the latest problem or issue. Though this was a natural part of his personality, it was also a conscious decision. He explained, "If I walk slowly through that plant with a frown on my face, people's fears will be triggered. They'll worry that we are about to close the plant or downsize. On the other hand, by walking through with a big smile and stopping to talk to people, I help to activate the positive. Tonight, some of these people will tell their families at dinner how the big guy from headquarters stopped to talk to them and that they explained to him how the new equipment was working. Their families will be proud of them. I know—I've been there. This is what leadership is all about."

The SEVEN ROLES of the Noble Business Leader

CEO stands for "Chief *Executive* Officer." Note the emphasis on "execution" right in the label for the corporation's top leader. Perhaps this phrase came about because historically the owner of a company brought in an outside manager to implement the owner's strategy or, in other words, to *execute* the owner's commands.

Today's CEO has a far larger role than merely execution. The Noble Leader takes on at least seven roles, each one important to the success of the enterprise.

1. Chief Reality Officer

As a start and continually along the way, leaders must assess reality. In a Noble Enterprise, this role has special prominence because Noble Leaders not only assess reality; they also define reality—in the process often redefining it or at least people's perception of it. This alone can have a dramatic effect on the success of the company.

Whenever an organization operates within its own (mistaken) reality rather than in the "real world," it has a hard time improving performance. Conversely, only when people first see and accept reality can they accomplish great leaps forward.

As Bill Catucci and his Unitel Deal Team sought ways to save that company, they shifted their mindset from the question "*Is* there a way to save Unitel?" to the question "*What* is the way to save it?" Only after they first believed that there *was* a way were they then able to *find* it.

Later, when Bill became CEO, he shared the message early on every time he met with the employees of Unitel that it was absolutely necessary to change. He did this by first describing the company as "on a burning platform" that needed to be abandoned if there was to be a future. Then he introduced his vision of a new, successful company and invited people to join in the adventure of building that company.

2. Chief Business Paradigm Officer

The Noble Leader reexamines the business model of the company that he leads and often redefines it in a new, more powerful way, frequently shaping it to a reality that others do not (yet) see.

By traditional measures of what makes a business successful, Costco, the No. 4 U.S. retailer, should be looking for a "white knight" to buy it out or at least be looking for a new CEO by now.† The company pays the highest wages in the retail industry, sells products below the prices of major competitors, and has no advertising budget or PR department, features that elicit criticism from Wall Street analysts who complain that the company could make more money if only management would lower their employee compensation.

The only problem is that Costco is doing just fine in terms of all the business measures that really matter: customer loyalty, employee morale and dedication, growth, and financial performance.

Jim Senegal, the company's founder and CEO, marches to the beat of a different drummer. His business model is built on people: how to serve people and how to motivate people. He has broken down the old compartmentalized views of employee compensation and marketing and integrated them in a new, more powerful way.

Noble Leaders see the deepest essence of an enterprise, and they see it in human terms. Then they create the forms that express that essence to make successful businesses. Senegal's realization that his employees could play an important role in attracting customers, not just serving them when they enter the store, is one example. Another is AT&T Canada LDS's replacement of the traditional silo

---

†As reported on an ABC 20/20 TV program in late 2005.

management structure with an Integrated Strategic Management System. Regrettably, people who see success achieved under such novel circumstances may shrug it off as a quirk or get lost in the details of a leader's specific actions and miss the bigger picture.

A major part of defining the business model is to determine the strategy the company will follow. Bill Catucci saw the task of developing strategy as one of his core roles. "We needed to come together with a strategy that answers the questions: Where are we going to be as a company? What's this marketplace like? What are our competitive strengths? Are we going to be the low quality with low price provider? Or are we going to be the high quality with high price provider? This had to be one of the first things I did."

3. Chief Growth Officer

The primary performance objective for the Noble Business Leader is long-term profitable growth. It is not profit maximization at any one particular point in time, which can be accomplished temporarily by cutting out all investment in the future. Nor is it growth for growth's sake. It is a balance of growth and profitability.

When asked about the view of some Wall Street critics who said that Costco could be more profitable if it paid its employees less, Jim Senegal remarked, "They are concerned about next quarter's financial results; I'm trying to build a healthy organization that will last far into the future."

Bill Catucci created a culture of continuous improvement. That meant not only continually finding ways to improve quality and service, but also ways to grow as a person. Hence, he created the AT&T Canada University, dedicated to helping employees achieve "life-long learning."

4. Chief Inspiration Officer

Defining reality and determining strategy is important, but a Noble Business Leader also inspires people with new visions of what is needed and what is possible, thus propelling them to new levels of performance.

The Noble Leader generates positive energy by being an energy infuser. While many traditional leaders have concentrated on being energy (and thus performance) extractors, noble leaders see their role as *infusing* the organization and its people with energy.

Noble Leaders are also energy *transformers*. While many traditional leaders think of themselves as problem-solvers, for that may be what got them promoted, Noble Leaders view their primary job as turning everyday energies into powerful, positive, and focused energies. Often this is a process of first permitting those energies to come forth. Noble Leaders find many ways to do this, including: modeling this expression of energy, putting teams together in a way that brings forth that energy, and celebrating success.

Bill Catucci, reflecting on what he learned about leadership from directing two consecutive successful corporate turnarounds (AT&T Canada LDS and Equifax), remarked, "I learned how much power the CEO really has—but also how little power he has. On the one hand, I found I couldn't really make people do anything, but as the CEO, I had a huge ability to inspire people."

5. Chief Resource Officer / Steward

The Noble Leader is a steward of the company's strategic resources, responsible for assuring the health and vitality of the company and all of its critical resources, including not just its financial capital, but also its Customer Capital and Human Capital.

Recall that one of the first things Bill Catucci did as CEO of Unitel/AT&T Canada LDS, despite its dire financial situation, was to send to every employee a check for $175 as a symbol of what they would accomplish together. This amounted to nearly a half million dollars. No financial analysis could justify such an "unnecessary" expenditure at that time. There was no immediate contribution to shareholder value, but this transfer of financial capital into Human Energy Capital (largely Spiritual Capital), helped to reinvigorate a workforce whose morale had reached the depths. This and other actions to build Human Capital ultimately paid off in large gains in shareholder value.

Underscoring the importance of the people of JetBlue Airways, David Neeleman, its founder and former CEO, has observed:

- It's so easy to look at the bottom line and forget about the people who made it happen.

- People ask, "How can we keep this going?" So, we spend a lot of time thinking about this. When we sold stock, I didn't want to take stock options. I don't need any more. If I took them, that would be less for our people. I took a small salary. I don't need the money, so I figured, why don't we create a fund to help our crew members who are in need, and I'll match what people give; it's important for me to set an example.

- I thought it important that everyone at JetBlue be able to own a piece of the rock. So we have a stock purchase plan for employees.

- At an orientation program, when people ask, "What are you going to do?" I tell them, "It's our company, what are we going to do?"

- It's important to let people know what a tremendous impact they are having.

- Our crew members are ambassadors for our company. It's important to have people proud to work for the company.†

Such practices work: sixty percent of JetBlue's customers come to them by word of mouth and only twenty percent by advertising. Notwithstanding its recent scheduling snafus and management shake up, JetBlue has been consistently one of the few profitable airlines.

6. Chief Servant Officer

The Noble Leader makes sure that all constituencies are served.

Bill Catucci adopted a "multiple stakeholders" philosophy. In the mission he created for AT&T Canada, he identified four groups of stakeholders in order of importance: First, customers, for without customers there is no business. Second, employees, for they are who ultimately determine the success of the business. Third, financial

---

†From an April 2003 speech to the Northwestern Transportation Center

shareholders, for they provide the financial capital (at some risk) to enable the business to function. Fourth, the community, for the business must ultimately benefit the broader society.

Hearkening back to his military days, Catucci saw the CEO's role as one of responsibility for all those he was leading and affecting. "Being the CEO is an awesome responsibility. Leadership is not just power. It is responsibility to all the people involved in the business."

Under intense financial pressures, CEOs can lose sight of whom they serve. The Board of Directors, the shareholders, Wall Street—all seem likely candidates for the CEO to serve first and foremost. Noble Leaders make an effort to keep in perspective the relative importance of those whom they are there to serve.

David Neeleman, while at JetBlue Airways, at the end of a talk in which he stressed the importance of serving employees, was asked how he explained to Wall Street his emphasis on serving the employee (versus the shareholder). His response: "We serve our *employees*, who serve our *customers*, who serve our shareholders."

7. Chief Integration Officer

The Noble Leader also has the role of making sure that everything ties together. The traditional leader manages all the pieces well and assumes that is enough to generate superior performance. Noble Leaders recognize that they must also stand back and see that the whole is working.

Bill Catucci saw that the CEO's role goes beyond developing strategy and running an organization. It is holistic. It is about core purpose (Why are we in business?) and about governance (How do we bring people together and lead them to bring out their best?). The CEO's role is to create the mental linkages that bring about alignment. Everything has to have a reason that relates to the larger mission and vision, which in turn must link to the company's constituencies (customers, employees, vendors, community, and shareholders); to business components (markets, products, services, and departments); and to management decisions (on strategies, policies, or investment) and actions. "Most of what we do has some purpose in mind, some rationale behind it.... Everything pulls together."

Conclusion

Noble Leaders tap not only their own Intellectual Capital, but also their Spiritual Capital—not only their Heads, but also their Hearts—in their leadership. Thus, just as effective leaders always learn about the market, the company, and business strategies, Noble Leaders also always seek to increase the power and capacity of their Heart, Emotions, and Will so that they can provide the leadership that not only makes good decisions, but also inspires people to achieve far beyond the norm, surprising themselves and others in the process.

Let's turn now to the actions that Noble Leaders take to unleash the huge potential of their people and to lead their organizations to higher, undreamed of levels of performance.

CHAPTER 15

TEN STEPS FOR BUILDING A NOBLE ENTERPRISE

"Do not go where the path may lead, go instead where there is no path and leave a trail."

—Ralph Waldo Emerson

As a leader, you can start today to turn your organization into a Noble Enterprise. If you are not yet the leader, but want someday to build a Noble Enterprise, today you can begin to build the leadership "muscles" of a Noble Leader and use those muscles to help the organization of which you are a part to function more nobly and more effectively.

The actions of Noble Leaders succeed not just because they are the right thing to do but also because they are fueled by the energies of *who* the noble leader is. Thus the place where noble leaders start is with themselves.

The Noble Leader's "To Be" List

Leaders who seek to build Noble Enterprises not only have a "to do" list but also have a "to be" list, for they know that *who* they are matters just as much as what they *do*. Since their personal energy will ignite and fuel the development of a Noble Enterprise, they will need energy of the highest quality, freely flowing and focused. Using the "to be" list that follows, you can generate this energy:

Who is the authentic you?

Before you even work on designing your Noble Enterprise, start by taking the time to understand yourself. Who is the person deep within and not always revealed?

What do you stand for?

What qualities are so important in your life that you would put all your energy into creating a world characterized by these qualities?

What is your life's calling?

What is the reason you are here? Not just in terms of accomplishing material objectives but also down deep, in terms of your calling. What inner energies are you here to manifest and to ignite in others?

What energizes you?

What challenges, what situations, what kind of people bring out the best in you? And how do you recharge your own energies?

Unleashing the Energies of Mind and Heart

Throughout this book, we have explored and seen manifested the inner energies of success. To build and lead a noble enterprise, you need to strengthen and put to use the energies of your mind and heart.

Mind

In addition to learning all you can about your profession, your company, and your industry, develop and use the other powers of your mind—perception, and belief. To develop the beliefs and ways of seeing of a Noble Leader, continually take the time to:

1. See the ultimate purpose of the enterprise and always keep it in mind.
2. See the interconnection of all of the pieces and their effect on each other.
3. Believe in the nobility and capability of your people.

Heart

Besides using the powers of your Mind, awaken and use all the powers of your Heart, especially those of connection, caring, trust, and faith. To develop the heart of a Noble Leader, take the time to:

1. Be in touch with and act from your own sense of deepest purpose.
2. Connect with all people involved in an endeavor, even your adversaries.
3. Be grateful for the opportunity to serve in your leadership capacity.
4. See and embrace the goodness and greatness in all of the people with whom you work.

The Noble Leader's "To Do" List

Noble leaders take many actions to energize their companies and lead them to success. Here are ten major ones that you can start doing right now. Take note, however: these ten steps are most effective when you are also working on your own "to be" list and engaging the energies of Mind and Heart.

1. Create and champion a compelling purpose.

Most companies run on a fraction of available energy because they do not address the nonmaterial needs and aspirations of their employees, customers, vendors, and strategic partners.

Having a compelling purpose, one that inspires and excites people, making them proud to be part of the company, stimulates and focuses the energy of the organization. By pursuing a powerful vision and mission that speaks to both material and nonmaterial purposes, the Noble Enterprise attracts and retains good people and inspires them to bring forth the best of their energy.

Setting cost targets or profit goals is not enough; the human dimension is especially important. You need to be able to say why your company is in business. Yes, it's to make and sell a product or service, but people need more than that. They want meaning in their work, and Noble Enterprises give it to them. The more you answer "Why?" not only in materialistic terms but also in emotional and spiritual terms, the higher will be the motivation and commitment of your team—and customers and suppliers too.

The vision Bill Catucci created for Unitel/AT&T Canada attracted the new talent (primarily from within the company) that he needed and kept stars from leaving early in the turnaround. It also brought hope and excitement to employees long discouraged, lacking in confidence and energy.

2. Hire people with character and passion as well as knowledge and skills.

All leaders seek to hire people with the necessary skills and knowledge. Noble Enterprises also focus on character to make sure that the people they hire have the motivation, the relationship skills, and the passion needed for the company to succeed.

Employees' character is a major source of a Noble Enterprise's sustainable competitive advantage. Noble Enterprises shape hiring and operating practices to attract, utilize, and promote people with the character they want for their businesses. By emphasizing character as well as talent, they create an unbeatable company.

Southwest Airlines, one of the country's most admired companies, hires for attitude (an important aspect of character) and trains for skills. During the slowdown right after September 11, 2001, the airline industry laid off over 100,000 employees. Only one major U.S. airline did not lay off employees: Southwest, which also was the only profitable major airline.

All too often what seems like a lackluster group of employees will be sent packing because senior executives believe they are seeing the manifestation of a lack of skill or motivation or passion. Yet the replacements often fail to perform as well. It is not so much that better people are needed as that a better culture and leadership are needed to turn these people on.

When Bill Catucci left AT&T Canada, he went to Equifax to lead a turnaround of that company. Despite being advised to clean house, Bill chose instead to keep all of the management people he inherited. Together, they created over $3 billion of new shareholder value in three years (and during a stagnant stock market)!

So, for your own organization, hire people who bring *all* of themselves to work, not just their minds, but also their emotions, their heart, and their will. When you have people working for your company who bring all of themselves to work, they achieve more, they grow more, they stay, and they contribute to making your company successful.

3. Make culture a competitive advantage.

In an interview with the Wall Street Journal, *Herb Kelleher, then CEO of Southwest Airlines, was asked, "You've often said that culture is your biggest competitive advantage. What do you mean?" He answered, "The intangibles are more important than the tangibles. Someone can go out and buy airplanes from Boeing and put up ticket counters, but they can't buy our culture, our esprit de corps."*

Values are not a new idea, but many companies are still only scratching the surface on how to capitalize on them to build companies that attract and retain not only great employees, but also great customers and suppliers. When companies select impressive values but do not live them, people become skeptics. By contrast, Noble Enterprises hardwire values into their organization.

They include them in their decision-making processes, sales strategies, customer service practices, employee development and evaluation processes, and measurement and reward systems.

A noble culture pays off not only in the successful performance of companies, but also in the motivation and retention of staff. When unfair policies and practices are rampant, people shut down, stop taking risks, and leave their best at home. Or they join the fray and use their energy against others, thus bringing out the worst in everyone.

Recall the headhunter who confided in AT&T Canada's HR director, Judy McLeod, "We could never get anyone out of your company," to which Judy replied, "That's because we created a culture people did not want to leave."

Build a culture of civility and respect. Set examples by your own personal conduct and by your company's practices. Do not tolerate acts of unfairness or incivility toward your employees, even from customers. By building a culture of civility, you will tap not only Intellectual Capital, but also Spiritual Capital.

4. Set big goals and call on people to rise to new levels.

Conventional wisdom says: Don't set goals that people might not be able to achieve, because if they fail to reach them, they will get discouraged. Instead, just ask them to "try hard" and "do their best." Noble Enterprises take a different path. They know that when the goal is important enough, people will respond. But great performance doesn't just happen; people must want to achieve high goals.

AT&T Canada LDS's mission and goals were lofty even by the standards of successful companies. For a company near death, losing a million dollars a day as well as customers and good staff in droves, its goals seemed unreachable. Yet, in large part because the goals and vision were big—and the CEO kept showing people they could achieve them—the company came back to life.

Thus, when you set a big goal, are passionate about this goal, communicate why it is important, and call on people to join you in the exciting endeavor to achieve it, people's energy eventually shifts into high gear. Help people develop and understand strategies and actions for achieving the goal and reporting the progress being made toward it. This will show people they can do it and will give them the confidence to reach even higher.

5. Use inner as well as outer goals and rewards.

In most companies, people focus primarily on the task at hand, on their "to do" lists. Often lost and overshadowed is the "Why are we doing this?" and the "What does it all mean anyway?"

Noble Enterprises communicate regularly and powerfully about their companies' purpose, direction, and strategy.

The management team of AT&T Canada LDS set goals for and developed strategies for improving employee morale, because they knew that one of the most important drivers of a successful business is the morale of its people. How could a company whose people had low morale ever hope to turn disaster into excellence? Thus, the heavy emphasis on finding ways to improve that morale. A second "inner" emphasis was on the company's values. Business decisions were made based on values. Employees and leaders were evaluated and rewarded based on how well they lived those values.

Take the time to set inner goals as well as outer goals. If you are leading a project team, for example, you might say, "Here is what we have to accomplish," and "Let's talk about how we will do it in a way that brings out the best in people, that builds more knowledge and skills, that builds our ability to work collaboratively—and that is fun." By paying attention to these aspects, you will actually succeed better and faster.

6. Give people an opportunity to grow.

In most companies, management is focused so much on *extracting* the most from employees—the most effort, the most creativity, the most performance—that they don't think much about helping them to increase their knowledge and skills. Providing such opportunities for employees seems like a luxury we cannot afford; the mentality is just to *get people with the right skills and get them working.* Yet, the AT&T Canada LDS case and other research shows that people want to expand and use new skills.

CEO Bill Catucci wanted people to improve themselves. His approach included creating an AT&T Canada University for life-long learning. It also included creating an atmosphere of professional and personal growth, in which people have considerable responsibility. *"I can't watch three thousand people. I'm going to give them the foundation and the values and hope that we're aligned. Then they're independent, they're on their own. They're going to do their thing, and you know what? Sometimes that works. They come out better than you had expected, and they've done it on their own, and they feel better about themselves. That is the model. Get them the tools to work with, so they can do what they want, which is to better themselves professionally and personally. By doing so, they improve the company."*

Provide opportunities for personal and professional growth for your employees—and invite them to use those new skills to achieve more and advance in your company. It will pay big dividends.

7. Create and lead a governance system that balances freedom and structure.

An oppressive management style prevents companies from using Human Capital to its full advantage. Stifled people do not bring their best to work. They do not innovate, they do not take risks, and they do not act with courage and self-confidence.

On the other hand, people do need some structure, so Noble Enterprises provide overall direction. But then to draw forth the best, these leaders give employees the freedom to take responsibility, to improvise, and to lead within that structure.

Most management systems encourage the "silo" approach to managing. Each function and division report to the CEO, who spends time with the head of each function and then is caught in between, having to run around dealing with conflicts in strategy and programs. By contrast, the Noble Enterprise fosters management focus, integration, and collaboration; swift decision-making; and coordinated implementation.

At AT&T Canada LDS, Bill Catucci created an Integrated Strategic Management System. When you look closely at most companies, he observed, "You'll find that people won't tell you what the governance system is because they won't have one. It will be very sketchy. My background and discipline forces me to have to do this. Then I can operate in a more flexible way."

Create a management process for your company that reflects the reality that the company is as much about human energy as it is about material form—a management process that promotes a holistic view of issues and strategies; generates collaboration among top executives, departments, and individuals; streamlines the strategy development process and integrates it with strategy implementation; and keeps the entire organization focused on what is most important.

8. Measure what really drives performance.

Most companies generate volumes of financial performance data and other outer measures, like product quality, customer retention, and employee turnover. In many companies, especially those that are doing poorly financially, there is so much focus on financial variables that management sometimes takes actions that harm the company's *inner* resources, such as customer satisfaction and employee morale, which are crucial to the long-term health and success of the company.

Performance on *inner* measures is actually a leading indicator of the more readily measured *outer*, or bottom line, measures. A downturn in customer retention, for example, is often preceded by a downturn in customer satisfaction. Similarly, today's employee morale levels affect future employee productivity and turnover.

AT&T Canada LDS surveyed employees annually to assess morale and understand its determinants. They developed strategies and actions regarding any aspect of morale that was low. And they used those surveys with leaders of individual units, so that those leaders could see how they were doing and take corrective actions to raise morale. They were evaluated on how well they did this.

Create measures of both material performance and nonmaterial performance. Then take the time with your people to analyze and understand all performance measures and to develop strategies, set goals, and take actions that will improve performance.

9. Communicate in both directions.

People want and need to hear about what management is doing and why, and they also want to know management's appraisal of employee performance.

Bill Catucci created a newsletter for AT&T Canada LDS which included news about employees, focusing on their successes, and also a column written by Bill about the company, often explaining the company's strategy or what was going on in the quality movement or with customers.

But communication is more than just making pronouncements and conveying management's latest decisions. It is two-way, both listening to employees and responding. *Bill also took the time to visit remote locations of AT&T Canada LDS to give presentations updating people about the company and to meet with and assist small groups and individual employees.*

So, in your own leadership, make sure that important goals, strategies, values, and results are all communicated—and in several ways and several times—and with positive energy. Conversely, make sure you send the message—not just in word, but also in action—that you are open to receiving communication back.

10. Celebrate

One of the biggest energy generators is celebration, an acknowledgment that people have achieved something important. People want to feel appreciated. They also want to know they are making a difference. Celebrations emphasize the positive and honor people's efforts and success, which in turn generates enthusiasm, confidence, and the commitment to reach even higher.

The management team at AT&T Canada LDS found many ways to celebrate publicly the progress the company was making, for example publicizing the progress in quality improvement and winning of a quality award and holding a public ceremony marking the opening of the AT&T Canada University. These celebrations became both a form of reward and recognition and a confidence booster for going after even bigger goals.

When you set important goals and have good measures and use them, you will know what you can celebrate and when. Take time to stop and acknowledge success and share the feeling of joint accomplishment.

Take a few minutes to review this list—perhaps also sharing it with others in your organization—and pick a few of the ten steps described here that you will consciously build into your organization (and your leadership). Once you start seeing the shift in energy, you'll want to do even more.

ON THE PATH TO UPLIFTING PEOPLE AND PROFITS

Noble Business Enterprises are well positioned to succeed on many levels. They:

- provide an uplifting and inspiring work environment for those who want to grow and contribute materially, intellectually, and spiritually
- serve customers at the highest level
- serve society, not just at a material level, but also at a nonmaterial, spiritual level
- provide superior returns to financial shareholders.

The inner essence of your Noble Enterprise may be invisible to the traditional eye, but it is the true engine of your enterprise. The inner essence doesn't concern itself only with dramatic outer actions, but rather focuses more on powerful inner forces that contribute, for example, to a genuine connection with others, a presence, a deep commitment to noble purpose, and the serving of all.

By following the strategies and actions outlined above and throughout this book, you can create a Noble Enterprise, an organization full of energy, purpose, and spirit that generates uncommon and sustainable business performance. With careful nurturing, these gains then serve as the foundation for even further gains.

For in the end, the Noble Enterprise approach is a process that sets souls on fire.

Special Announcement

How You Can Start Applying Noble Enterprise Principles in Your Business

If you want to learn more about noble enterprise and how it can help you build a more successful business—with greater growth and profitability—and do it in a way that is not only ethical but that also attracts and retains the most passionate, motivated employees, we stand ready to help you, such as by providing information and guidance about the Noble Enterprise model, examples, and tools via our:

- € suggestions for using the *Noble Enterprise* book in your company to introduce Noble Enterprise approaches
- € *Leadership in a New Light* newsletter
- € Notes on Noble Business blog
- € other publications
- € public presentations and seminars
- € consulting or coaching assistance

To learn more, please visit a special Web page for readers of this book:

www.NobleBusinessSolutions.com/LearnMore

An Invitation to Noble Enterprise Practitioners:

How You Can Help Advance the Noble Enterprise Business Model

If you lead or are part of a Noble Enterprise, whether it be a large corporation or a small firm, we invite you to share the good news about your company:

- € how you lead your company in ways that attract and inspire exceptional employees
- € how your serve your customers
- € how you create financial performance far beyond the norm
- € what Noble Enterprise principles you use with what results

You and others like you are uplifting the fundamental nature of business and, in the process, are changing the world for the better. To learn how you can participate in spreading the word about the power of Noble Enterprise to turn ordinary businesses into great places to work, to do business with, and to invest in, please visit:

www.NobleBusinessSolutions.com/ParticipateInNE

Contact information:
e-mail: info@NobleBusinessSolutions.com
phone: 800-781-3147 (USA)
Web site: www.NobleBusinessSolutions.com

ACKNOWLEDGMENTS

Many people helped make this book possible through their insights, their example, their inspiration, and their encouragement.

My parents emphasized that it was not just what one *accomplished* that mattered; that what mattered even more was *how* one lived life and interacted with others.

Wise, inspiring faculty challenged me early to think for myself and question conventional wisdom—at Hotchkiss, at Yale in economics but also in philosophy courses that encouraged exploration and tapping my own wisdom, and then at the University of Chicago by such luminaries as Milton Friedman and George Stigler, both Noble laureates.

In my early years in corporate America (in the late 1960s and early 1970s), I was blest to work for Bob Moore, trained as an accountant but at heart a people person, who rose quickly into financial management positions within Union Carbide. Besides becoming a valued mentor (and later a client), Bob also provided an early and vivid example of managing as if people mattered. Under his guidance, I felt free to explore and get involved in issues and ideas beyond the traditional.

Later, in the mid 1970s, I worked as a senior consultant at Schaffer Associates, a leading midsize consulting firm, where I learned from Bob Schaffer, Ron Ashkenas, and their colleagues how to help clients translate management principles into action that generated high performance.

In 1980, Don Ketcham, the minister of my church, invited me to help start a group of business people in the church to explore the notion of putting our religious beliefs into action in our business roles. This experience deepened my interest in the spiritual aspects of leadership and of organizations, and led to my giving talks at several churches on Heart Power and even at a business association meeting.

As I began exploring human-centered models of business and leadership in the 1980s and became involved in various spirit at work organizations, I met people who provided both inspiration and encouragement. This included Gordon Davidson (Center for Visionary Leadership) with whom I collaborated to explore and give talks about the inner energies of corporations, and also Virginia Swain, Joseph Baratta, Tom Hansen, Jim Davidson, Ron and Randi Nelson, Cynthia Belden, and many others who share a vision of a people- and earth-friendly business world.

In the 1990s, Judi Neal, founder of the International Center for Spirit at Work, provided an opportunity to share early versions of my energy-based business model with PhD students in her research course at the University of New Haven. Later George Starcher provided encouragement and an opportunity to present my emerging concept of spiritual capital at several annual conferences of the European Baha'i Business Forum.

I am grateful to Professor Severyn Bruyn of Boston College, who reviewed an early draft in the mid 1990s and provided encouragement to press on regarding the economic concepts I was developing. Barbara Williams, CEO of Image Content Technology, encouraged my efforts to integrate the spiritual and financial dimensions in my new business model, and provided unflagging encouragement to finish the book as well as valued consultation when the going got rough.

Thanks also to members of a group of business owners and corporate executives that Carol Coutrier (the Launching Pad) and I led in the late 1990s to explore the role of the inner, spiritual aspects of leadership. These members, each in their own way, personified the qualities of noble leadership eventually described in the book (and also in our In a New Light newsletter), notably, Mary Lou Andre (Dressing Well), Steve Hall (Chandler Associates), David Wood (who at the time was an executive with Bose), Ken Boroson (Boroson Architects), and Ralph Levy (Quant Engineering Co). Thanks to Carol for her early and continued support of the book.

Thanks to Lauren Holmes, who opened my eyes to the possible, and provided practical and inspiring guidance in expanding my horizons. Thanks also to Sue Smith, who gave her time and experience to help me and several others create the Institute for Human Economics to explore human-centered economics and to offer information and inspiration to those who visited our Web site.

I am grateful to these clients, who provided examples of Noble Enterprise and Noble Leadership over the past several decades, including: Jim Broadhead (then of St. Joe Minerals), George Grune (Reader's Digest), Peter Habley (Pfizer), Bob Moore (Union Camp), Steve Hall (Chandler Associates), David Wood (then of Bose), and Brian Laughlin (Applied Wholesale Mortgage).

If this book proves inspiring to business owners and executives, it will be in large part because of the story of the Unitel/AT&T Canada Long Distance Services turnaround. The leaders and others in this company gave generously of their time and insights as I interviewed them about their experience of the company's (and their own) revitalization.

They are all mentioned in the book, but I'd like to give special thanks here to:

- *Bill Catucci*, who besides providing detailed information and reflections about the turnaround, also took the time to dialogue extensively about his views of leadership, to encourage completion of the book—and later to collaborate in making presentations and participating in a seminar on Noble Enterprise;

- *Renato Discenza*, one of the natural leaders whom Bill discovered within the organization, working on his own (even before Bill became CEO) to introduce enlightened leadership approaches and training. Renato provided considerable insights into the workings of the company's unique management system.

- *Karen Jeisi*, who played several different important roles in the turnaround, from project leader of the AT&T "Unitel Deal Team" that analyzed the Unitel situation and developed the plan to save and revitalize the company, to becoming a member of the board of AT&T Canada LDS. Karen provided considerable help both in the development of the story and in fact checking and review of various drafts of the story. She too has collaborated in presenting the Noble Enterprise seminar.

Lucille Meltz provided encouragement and coaching as I worked to turn my interview notes regarding the turnaround into chapters of the book. Her combination of gentle support and strong discipline proved invaluable in completing those chapters.

I am grateful to Amy Domini of Domini Social Investments, who provided the opportunity to meet with the analysts of DSI to discuss the Noble Enterprise model and to compare it with their methods of identifying candidates for inclusion in the DSI funds.

Ken Bardach of Olin School of Business provided early and continued encouragement in writing the book—and also invited me (along with Bill Catucci and Karen Jeisi of AT&T Canada LDS) to lead a seminar on Noble Enterprise for the world-renowned executive education program at Olin Business School at Washington University in St. Louis. With his reverence for the inner, spiritual dimension of life and work, Ken was a natural to write the Foreword, for which I am extremely grateful.

Thanks to Zoe Marae, who has provided valuable insights on the physics of human energy that contributed to my views of how this book may fit into a larger context of human evolution. Thanks also to Susan Stanton Rotman, who provided counsel at various forks in the road to bringing this book into the world.

I benefited greatly from participating in a book development program led by John Eggen of Mission Marketing Mentors, and from teaming up with my "writing partner" Joe Bavonese (The Relationship Institute) to coach each other regarding our writing projects. Both John and Joe also provided valuable perspective on markets and marketing.

I am deeply grateful to Alis Valencia, strategic editor, who (as an editor at Berrett-Koehler Publishers) reviewed an early version of the book, providing positive feedback about my model of the energized enterprise, then provided encouragement over the years, including publishing my article "Bringing a Company Back to Life: The Role of the CEO" (in a June 1999 *At Work* journal issue) introducing the AT&T Canada LDS story and my concept of spiritual capital, and eventually guided me in shaping the book, helping to organize it and to edit the content into a form that is far more readable than earlier versions. Thanks also to Karen Speerstra, who (as an editor at Butterworth-Heinemann publishers) also provided early support and then later some editing input.

Melanie McMillan played an important role in developing and implementing marketing strategies. Her instincts and enthusiasm have made a positive difference.

I am grateful to Judi Jones, who worked tirelessly behind the scenes, at one level to keep me focused on *completing* what seemed like a permanently ongoing writing project, and on another level to serve as project manager in taking care of countless details to finish the book and its various components.

Thanks also to the Cosimo Books team—Alex Dake and MaryAnn Johanson—who turned it all into the book you have before you.

Finally thanks to close friends and family, who continually encouraged, cajoled, and pushed me when I wandered away from the book to pursue other seemingly important endeavors, to get me back to writing the book, particularly my wife, Barbara, who shares the passion for discovering and traveling the inner, spiritual path as well as enjoying its outer manifestations.

SUGGESTED READING

Aburdene, Patricia. *Megatrends 2010: The Rise of Conscious Capitalism.* Hampton Roads Publishing Company, New Ed edition 2007.

Argyris, Chris. *Overcoming Organizational Defenses: Facilitating Organizational Leaarning.* Prentice Hall, March 1990.

Argyris, Chris; Bennis, Warren G; and Thomas, Robert J. *Harvard Business Review on Developing Leaders (Harvard Business Review Paperback Series).* Harvard Business School Press, February 2004.

Ashkenas, Ron (et al.). *The Boundaryless Organization: Breaking the Chains of Organization Structure.* Jossey-Bass, October 1998.

Barrett, Richard. *Liberating the Corporate Soul: Building a Visionary Organization.* Butterworth-Heinemann, 1998.

Becker, Gary. *Human Capital.* University of Chicago Press, 1994.

Bennis, Warren. *On Becoming a Leader: The Leadership Classic—Updated and Expanded.* Perseus Publishing, Revised edition, 2003.

Blanchard, Kenneth and Johnson, Spencer. *The One Minute Manager.* HarperCollins Business, 2000.

Blanchard, Kenneth; Lacinak, Thad; Tompkins, Chuck; and Ballard, Jim. *Whale Done!: The Power of Positive Relationships.* Free Press, 2002.

Block, Peter. *Stewardship.* Berrett-Koehler Publishers, 1993.

Bohman, Lee G. and Deal, Terrance E. *Leading with Soul.* Jossey-Boss Publishers, 1995.

Bossidy, Larry; Charan, Ram; and Lloyd, John Bedford. *Execution: The Discipline of Getting Things Done.* Crown Publishing Group, 2002.

Bruyn, Severyn T. *A Civil Economy: Transforming the Market in the Twenty-First Century.* Michigan, 2000.

Buckingham, Marcus and Coffman, Curt. *First, Break All The Rules: What the World's Greatest Managers Do Differently.* Simon and Schuster, 1999.

Burns, James MacGregor. *Transforming Leadership: A New Pursuit of Happiness.* Grove/Atlantic, Inc, February 2003.

Capra, Fritjof. *The Tao of Physics: An Exploration of the Parallels Between Modern Physics and Eastern Mysticism.* Editorial Sirio, 1983.

Cashman, Kevin. *Leadership from the Inside Out*. Executive Excellence Publishing, 2001.

Chappell, Tom. *The Soul of a Business: Managing for Profit and the Common Good*. Bantam Books, 1993.

Chouinard, Yvon. *Let My People Go Surfing: The Education of a Reluctant Businessman*. Penguin Press HC, 2005.

Collins, James. *Built to Last: Successful Habits of Visionary Companies*. Harper Business, 1994.

Collins, Jim. *Good to Great: Why Some Companies Make the Leap...and Others Don't*. HarperCollins Publishers, October 2001.

Conley, Chip. *Peak: How Great Companies Get Their Mojo from Maslow*. Jossey-Bass, 2007.

Covey, Stephen. *Principle-Centered Leadership*. Free Press, 1st edition, 1992.

Covey, Stephen. *The 7 Habits of Highly Effective People*. Free Press, 2004.

Covey, Stephen. *Everyday Greatness*. Thomas Nelson, 2006.

De Geus, Arie. *The Living Company*. Harvard Business School Press, 1st edition, 2002.

De Pree, Max. *Leadership Is an Art* and *Leading Without Power*. Doubleday Business, 2004.

Derber, Charles. *People Before Profit: The New Globalization in an Age of Terror, Big Money, and Economic Crisis*. Picador, 2003.

Dolan, Paul and Elkjer, Thom. *True to Our Roots: Fermenting a Business Revolution*. Bloomberg Press, 2003.

Drucker, Peter. *Management Challenges for the 21st Century*. Collins, 1st edition, 2001.

Drucker, Peter. *Post-Capitalist Society*. Butterworth-Heinemann, New edition, November 1994.

Drucker, Peter. *The Effective Executive (and the Effective Executive in Action)*. Harper Business, 2006.

Eisler, Riane. *The Power of Partnership: Seven Relationships That Will Change Your Life*. New World Library, 2003.

Fogel, Robert. *The Fourth Great Awakening and the Future of Egalitarianism*. University of Chicago Press, 2000.

Fox, Matthew. *The Reinvention of Work: A New Vision of Livelihood for Our Time.* Harper Collins, 1994.

Friedman, Milton and Friedman, Rose. *Free to Choose: A Personal Statement.* Harvest Books, 1990.

Gillett, Darwin (contributing author). *Create the Business Breakthrough You Want: Secrets and Strategies from the World's Greatest Mentors.* Mission Publishing, 2004.

Gillett, Darwin. "Moving Beyond the 'Either Or' of Human Spirit and Profits." *Inspire EBBF,* January 2006.

Gillett, Darwin. "Bringing a Company Back to Life: The Role of a CEO." *At Work Journal,* May/June 1999.

Gillett, Darwin. "That's the Spirit: Sharing the Wealth of Corporate Energy." *Business Spirit Journal,* October/November 1997.

Gillett, Darwin. "Rebuilding the Human Spirit After Downsizing." *PIMA Magazine,* December 1996.

Goldratt, Eliyahu. *The Goal: A Process of Ongoing Improvement.* North River Press, 1992.

Greenleaf, Robert; Spears, Larry C.; and Covey, Stephen R. *Servant Leadership.* Paulist Press, 2002.

Greider, William. *The Soul of Capitalism: Opening Paths to a Moral Economy.* Simon & Schuster Inc., 2003.

Hawkins, David R. *Power vs. Force: The Hidden Determinants of Human Behavior.* Hay House, 2002.

Hazlitt, Henry. *Economics in One Lesson.* Three Rivers Press, 1988.

Henderson, Hazel. *Building A Win-Win-World: Life Beyond Economic Warfare.* Berrett-Koehler Publishers, New Ed edition, 1997.

Hollick, Malcolm. *The Science of Oneness: A Worldview for the Twenty-First Century.* O Books, 2006.

Holmes, Lauren. *Peak Evolution: Beyond Peak Performance and Peak Experience.* Naturality Net, 2001.

Johnson, Spencer and Blanchard, Kenneth. *Who Moved My Cheese? An Amazing Way to Deal with Change in Your Work and in Your Life.* G. P. Putnam's Sons, 1998.

Kaplan, Robert S. and Norton, David P. *The Balanced Scorecard: Translating Strategy into Action*. Harvard Business School Press, September 1996.

Kise, Jane A. G. and Stark, David. *Working With Purpose: Finding a Corporate Calling For You and Your Business*. Augsburg Fortress Publishers, August 2004.

Kofman, Fred. *Conscious Business: Transforming Your Workplace (And Yourself) by Changing the Way You Think, Act, and Communicate*. Sounds True, 2002.

Kohn, Alfie. *No Contest: The Case Against Competition*. Houghton Mifflin, 1986.

Kotter, John. *John P. Kotter on What Leaders Really Do*. HBS, Harvard Business Review Book, 1999.

Kotter, John. *Leading Change*. Harvard Business School Press, 1996.

Jaworski, Joseph; Flowers, Betty S.; and Senge, Peter. *Synchronicity: The Inner Path of Leadership*. Berrett-Koehler, 1996.

Kouzes, James and Posner, Barry Z. *The Leadership Challenge*. Jossey-Bass Inc., 2003.

Krames, Jeffrey A. *Jack Welch and the 4 E's of Leadership*. McGraw-Hill, 2005.

Marcic, Dorothy. *Managing with the Wisdom of Love*. Jossey-Bass, 1st edition, 1997.

Maslow, Abraham. *Motivation and Personality*. HarperCollins Publishers, 1954.

Maslow, Abraham. *Toward a Psychology of Being*. Wiley, 1968.

Maxwell, John. *Developing the Leader Within You*. Thomas Nelson, 2001.

McKibben, Bill. *Deep Economy: The Wealth of Communities and the Durable Future*. Times Books, 2007.

McTaggart, Lynne. *The Field: The Quest for the Secret Force of the Universe*. Harper Collins, 2001.

Miller, Larry. *Competing in the New Capitalism: How Individuals, Teams and Companies Are Creating the New Currency of Wealth*. AuthorHouse, 2006.

Myss, Caroline. *Anatomy of the Spirit: The Seven Stages of Power and Healing*. Crown Publishers Inc., 1996.

Neal, Judi. *Edgewalkers: People and Organizations That Take Risks, Build Bridges, and Break New Ground*. Praeger Publishers, 2006.

Neuschel, Robert. *The Servant Leader: Unleashing the Power of Your People*. Vision Sports Management Group Inc., 1998.

Peters, Tom. *Re-imagine! Business Excellence in a Disruptive Age.* Better Life Media Inc., 2006.

Pfeffer, Jeffrey. *The Human Equation: Building Profits by Putting People First.* Harvard Business School Press; 1998.

Porras, Jerry; Emery, Stewart; and Thompson, Mark. *Success Built to Last: Creating a Life That Matters.* Wharton School Publishing, 2006.

Porter, Michael E. *Competitive Advantage: Creating and Sustaining Superior Performance.* Free Press, 1985.

Pottruck, David S. and Pearce, Terry. *Clicks and Mortar: Passion Driven Growth in an Internet Driven World.* Jossey–Bass, 2nd edition, 2001.

Rabbin, Robert. *Invisible Leadership: Igniting the Soul at Work.* Acropolis Books, 1998.

Renesch, John. *Leadership in a New Era: Visionary Approaches to the Biggest Crisis of Our Times* and *The New Bottom Line: Bringing Heart and Soul to Business.* New Leaders Press, 1994.

Ressler, Peter & Ressler, Monika Mitchell. *Spiritual Capitalism: What the FDNY Taught Wall Street About Money.* Chilmark Books, 2005.

Ridley, Matt. *The Origins of Virtue: Human Instincts and the Evolution of Cooperation.* Viking, 1997

Schaffer, Robert. *The Breakthrough Strategy: Using Short-Term Success to Build the High-Performance Organizations.* Collins, New Ed edition, 1990.

Schwerin, David. *Conscious Capitalism: Principles for Prosperity.* Butterworth Heinemann, 1998.

Secretan, Lance. *Inspire! What Great Leaders Do.* Wiley, April 2004.

Secretan, Lance. *ONE: The Art and Practice of Conscious Leadership.* The Secretan Center Inc., 2006.

Secretan, Lance. *Reclaiming Higher Ground: Creating Organizations That Inspire the Soul.* The Secretan Center Inc., 2003.

Senge, Peter M. *The Fifth Discipline: The Art & Practice of the Learning Organization.* Currency Doubleday, 1990.

Stephen, Michael. *Spirituality in Business: The Hidden Success Factor.* Inspired Productions Press LLC, 2002.

Stewart, Thomas A. *Intellectual Capital: The New Wealth of Organizations,* Currency Doubleday, 1997.

Tapscott, Don and Williams, Anthony. *Wikinomics: How Mass Collaboration Changes Everything*. Penguin Group, 2006.

Torbert, William R. *Action Inquiry: The Secret of Timely and Transforming Leadership.* Berrett-Koehler Publishers, 2004.

Warren, Rick. *The Purpose-Driven Life: What On Earth Am I Here For?* Inspirio/Zondervan Miniature Editions, 2003.

Wheatley, Margaret. *Leadership and the New Science.* Berrett-Koehler, 1992.

Whitney, John O. *The Trust Factor: Liberating Profits & Restoring Corporate Vitality.* McGraw-Hill, 1993.

Yankelovich, Daniel. *Profit with Honor. The New Stage of Market Capitalism.* Yale University Press, 2007.

Zukav, Gary. *The Dancing Wu Li Masters: An Overview of the New Physics.* Harper Perennial Modern Classics, 2001.

INDEX

ABOUT THE AUTHOR

Darwin Gillett is a consultant to corporate management and business owners on strategies for revitalizing their organizations, creating competitive advantage, and achieving sustainable growth and profitability.

Gillett speaks widely in North America and Europe on leadership strategies for creating sustainable competitive advantage in knowledge-based and relationship-based companies through the principles of Noble Enterprise, which tap the full range of human talent and spirit. He also designs and leads executive development seminars on Noble Leadership for business schools, associations, and individual companies.

He has published numerous articles and booklets on business and leadership and is a contributing author to the 2004 book *Create the Business Breakthrough You Want: Secrets and Strategies from the World's Greatest Mentors.*

Gillett is founder and president of Noble Business Solutions, which helps clients revitalize their companies' growth and profitability. As a business strategist, corporate futurist, and leadership coach, he consults with business owners and corporate executives and their teams on strategies for achieving sustainable breakthrough performance. His corporate clients have included large multinational companies such as Bose, Dixie Northern (Georgia Pacific), Pfizer, Reader's Digest, St Joe Minerals, Union Camp (now part of International Paper), and Union Carbide (now part of Dow). Privately held clients include firms in high tech and professional services, including law, engineering, construction management, architecture, real estate, and high-end software.

Gillett holds a BA in economics from Yale University and an MBA from the University of Chicago Graduate School of Business. He serves on several business and nonprofit boards and has lectured at several graduate-level business schools, including Dartmouth's Tuck School of Business, Washington University's Olin Business School, and Fordham University's Graduate School of Business.

Gillett lives on the coast of Maine with his wife, where he enjoys the region's seashore, lakes and mountains and from which he draws inspiration for writing about business leadership and providing consulting advice and coaching support to his clients.

For more information about Gillett's work and Noble Business Solutions, please visit www.NobleBusinessSolutions.com.

COSIMO

COSIMO is a specialty publisher of books and publications that inspire, inform, and engage readers. Our mission is to offer unique books to niche audiences around the world.

COSIMO BOOKS publishes books and publications for innovative authors, nonprofit organizations, and businesses. **COSIMO BOOKS** specializes in bringing books back into print, publishing new books quickly and effectively, and making these publications available to readers around the world.

COSIMO CLASSICS offers a collection of distinctive titles by the great authors and thinkers throughout the ages. At **COSIMO CLASSICS** timeless works find new life as affordable books, covering a variety of subjects including: Business, Economics, History, Personal Development, Philosophy, Religion & Spirituality, and much more!

COSIMO REPORTS publishes public reports that affect your world, from global trends to the economy, and from health to geopolitics.

FOR MORE INFORMATION CONTACT US AT
INFO@COSIMOBOOKS.COM

- if you are a book lover interested in our current catalog of books
- if you represent a bookstore, book club, or anyone else interested in special discounts for bulk purchases
- if you are an author who wants to get published
- if you represent an organization or business seeking to publish books and other publications for your members, donors, or customers.

COSIMO BOOKS ARE ALWAYS AVAILABLE AT ONLINE BOOKSTORES

VISIT COSIMOBOOKS.COM
BE INSPIRED, BE INFORMED